Stud
in

Studying and living in Britain 1993

The British Council's guide for overseas students and visitors

Northcote House
in association with
The British Council

Text completely revised with new material by J E Melrose-Woodman 1984

Revised and updated 1992

First published 1949
This edition 1993

Published by Northcote House Publishers Ltd,
Plymbridge House, Estover Road, Plymouth PL6 7PZ, United Kingdom.
Tel: Plymouth (0752) 735251. Telex: 45635. Fax: (0752) 695699.

British Library Cataloguing in Publication Data
Studying and living in Britain 1993: the British Council's guide for overseas students and visitors.
1. Great Britain. Higher education institutions.
Foreign students
I. British Council
378.1982

ISBN 0-7463-0656-3

Typeset by PDQ Typesetting, Stoke-on-Trent

Printed in Great Britain by BPCC Wheatons Ltd, Exeter

Contents

Introduction

The aim of this book is to provide you, as a student coming to Britain from overseas, with some basic information on the educational, financial and social aspects of studying and living in Britain. Although mainly for those undertaking long-term study, the contents should also help short-term students and others such as business visitors and tourists.

The book has been arranged chronologically, taking events in the same order as they will happen to you. It has been designed to be of most help before you leave home and during your first few weeks in Britain. You will find that more detailed, local information will be given to you after you arrive by your sponsoring body and/or educational institution and also by various student organizations (sometimes in large confusing quantities). This 'first guide' should help you while you try to familiarize yourself with everything else.

Studying and Living in Britain is not a guide to the British educational system or to the courses available here. You may also find, if you have previously visited Britain, that you know some of what the book contains. On the other hand, if you have had very limited contact with Britain and the British people, there may be areas you would like covered in greater detail. Whatever you feel, we hope the specific guidance given in the main text and the bibliography of useful publications given at the end will tell you how to find whatever detailed information you need.

One particular organization that you should be aware of is the United Kingdom Council for Overseas Student Affairs (UKCOSA). Established in 1968, it is the UK's leading organization in the overseas student field. It is a national body which looks after the needs and promotes the interests of overseas students in the UK and of those who work with them. You can usually contact UKCOSA through the welfare officer or student adviser in your college or student union. For further advice and assistance before you leave home you should contact the nearest British Council office. Addresses of offices overseas are given in Appendix 1.

1
Deciding to come

In this chapter we try to answer all the questions you will be asking yourself before you finally decide to come to Britain.

WHAT STANDARD OF ENGLISH IS NEEDED?

English is one of the most widely spoken languages in the world and, as such, can be extremely useful both socially and professionally. It is more important than anything else, if your stay is to be a success, that you can speak, write and understand English well. Not only do you need to speak it well enough to find your way round cities, public transport, shops, libraries and other places and to hold conversations with people you meet but, more important, you must be fluent enough to follow lectures and contribute to discussions in your course of study, which will probably involve a much wider and often quite technical vocabulary. If you are not sufficiently fluent, the results of your course may be disappointing, reflecting your difficulties with the language rather than your ability in the subject.

For this reason, most universities and colleges will not accept you on a course without evidence of fluency in English. If you would like to check on the standard of your English, you can go to the British Council in your own country, where you can assess your fluency by taking the International English Language Testing System Test (IELTS). Most places of higher education in Britain recognize a score of six or above as an acceptable level for academic study.

If your English needs improving, it is obviously better to take a language course before leaving home. If this is not possible arrange, either in advance or as soon as you arrive, to join a course in Britain. Most local education authorities here run day or evening classes. The British Association of State Colleges in English Language Teaching (BASCELT) publishes a handbook which gives details of courses offered throughout the United Kingdom (address in Appendix 2). There are also plenty of private language schools which run courses, but their fees are usually higher than the state-run courses. You can get a list of private schools, which have been recognized as efficient by the British Council, from the Association for Recognized English Language Teaching Establishments (ARELS/FELCO) (address in Appendix 2) or from your local British Council office. The British Council publishes English Studies Information Service (ESIS) sheets on English language learning and teaching which are also available from your nearest British Council office; these include details of *Polytechnic and College Courses in English for Overseas Students, Summer and Short Courses in TEFL, EFL and ESP* and *Short Courses in TEFL, EFL and ESP.*

WHAT ARE THE COSTS?

Having money worries can mean the difference between success and failure in your chosen field and make you thoroughly miserable too. A Nigerian student, for example, who came to Britain to study in Bournemouth on the south coast wrote:

> 'Nigeria Government was in financial difficulty, hence my remittance delayed. Hopefully, I went to my principal and explained the matter. I was lent £100, and made to sign a document that repayment will be made within a month. Signing a document because of only £100! I feel as if I was stabbed at the heart and made me a depressed person... it was like me having a nightmare.'
>
> Ajayi, F. 'Money makes the difference' in: *Overseas students — at home in Britain?* UKCOSA 1987

To avoid money worries during your stay in Britain use the information we give you below to work out exactly what it will cost for your particular course, for the sort of place you would like to live in and for the sort of things you would like to be able to do.

COST OF THE COURSE

Most first-degree courses in the United Kingdom are three years in length so that overall costs may be less than in other countries where a degree course takes longer. Chart A (see page 9) will help you to make a rough calculation of the fees you can expect to pay. You would be wise, however, to confirm the exact amount of fees with your chosen college as soon as you can as some charge more than those in the chart. Nationals of the European Community (EC) who have been living in the EC for the three years immediately before the course starts are normally only charged fees at home-student rates. If you are an EC national applying for a first-degree course or equivalent and have not already done a similar course elsewhere, you may be eligible for reimbursement of your fees by the British government. For more information consult the college where you will be studying.

BASIC LIVING COSTS

In 1993 a single student living in London would need £570 per month (£6,840 per year) to meet basic living expenses: rent, heating, lighting, food, daily fares, medical cover and other necessities. In regions outside London, for example Newcastle-upon-Tyne in the North-East, Bristol in the South-West, Dundee in Scotland, Belfast in Northern Ireland and Aberystwyth in Wales, it costs from £380 to £500 per month (£4,560 to £6,000 per calendar year). It should be stressed, however, that these figures are all approximate and how much you actually spend will depend a lot on your personal life-style. Some people may be able to live more cheaply, others might find it hard to maintain their usual standard of living. Rent and medical cover are discussed in more detail in Chapter 4; the other elements are covered below.

CHART A: MINIMUM RECOMMENDED TUITION FEES FOR THE YEAR 1992/93

Universities	Students from EC member countries*	Students from non-EC member countries
Arts degreee courses	£1,855	£ 5,320
Science degree courses, including pre-clinical years of medicine, dentistry, and veterinary science	£2,770	£ 7,055
Clinical years of courses in medicine, dentistry and veterinary science	£4,985	£12,990
Postgraduate	£2,200	variable
Colleges: The Council of Local Education Authorities sets the minimum fees for advanced and non-advanced further education.		
Postgraduate	£2,104	variable
Non-designated higher education (i.e. first degrees, BTEC, HNDs and other advanced courses) Arts degrees Science degrees	} £759	} £5,319
Non-advanced further education (i.e. courses at a level below HND)	£570	£2,946
Polytechnics: from 1990/91 onwards minimum tuition fees have not been recommended for polytechnics.		

Note: Fees may vary from one institution to another and you should check with the institutions when you apply. Fees are likely to go up from year to year.

* Students must have been living in the EC for the three years before the start of the course, and can be nationals of an EC country.

Heating
Britain can be fairly cold for much of the year and students from hot countries may need heating for as long as eight months in the year. Cheap lodgings are not often centrally heated and gas or electric fires provided are usually controlled by coin meters. In very cold weather, you might have to put in as much as £2.40 in one evening; allow a minimum of £16.40 per week for heating in the winter.

Food
Based on a western-style diet of breakfast, a hot evening meal, and all meals at weekends eaten at home, plus £2.40 per day to cover your midday meal in the college canteen, a weekly cost of about £47.50 is likely.

Daily fares
Obviously these will vary depending on how far you live from the college and the shops. You can usually buy a season ticket; for example, in April 1991 a Travelcard covering three zones of the London Underground, London buses and British Rail trains cost £14.90 per week and for five zones £23.40.

Other basic necessities
To cover such items as launderette and dry-cleaning, toilet and household articles, stationery, stamps and telephone calls you would need about £12 per week.

Additions
Medical insurance for either six months or a year may be added (see page 42), so allow at least £90. Postgraduate students should include another £250 to £300 for the typing and binding of their theses; for a M.Phil./Ph.D. thesis the costs would be £400 to £650.

On top of your day-to-day living expenses, allocate an amount of money for initial expenses when you first arrive:

- books (assuming an intensive use of libraries). Up to £600.
- warm clothing (Chart D, page 51).
- deposits (e.g. for accommodation, see page 36). These can range from one week's to two months' rent.

All the amounts above are for a single student; if you are married with a family you will spend considerably more (see page 37).

ENTERTAINMENT

You will also need some money to follow interests beyond your academic studies. Even the most studious need time to relax and unwind and there are great social pressures on you from friends and acquaintances to do just this. Here is an idea of how much it might cost you.

Reading matter

daily newspaper	28p to 40p (Foreign language papers are more.)
magazines	45p to £2.50.
paperback books	£3.95 upwards (Books can be borrowed free from public libraries.)
cigarettes	£2.10– 2.30 per packet of twenty.

TV and radio

In a hall of residence there may be a communal television, and costs will probably be met by the college. However, if you live in a flat or house you may have to buy your own. A new colour television costs about £200–500 to buy, or £20 upwards (depending on the screen size) per month to rent. Second-hand sets are fairly easily obtained through advertisements placed in local newspapers. A licence is a legal requirement. For a black and white television it costs £26.50 per year and for a colour television £80.

Radios cost from £20 upwards, stereo equipment from £200, records and tapes from about £8.00 each and compact discs from £10 upwards. TV video films can be rented from £2 per night.

Sports

Many public sports facilities are subsidized by the state and can be used for a relatively small sum:

swimming	£1.30 to £2.00
squash	£2.20 to £3.50
tennis	£2.00 to £3.00

Museums and galleries

Britain is rich in museums and galleries and entrance is sometimes free.

Eating out

There is a large variety of places to eat out (more details in Chapter 8) but the following gives an idea of the range in cost:

	lunch	*dinner*
college canteen	£2.00	£3.00
inexpensive restaurant	£5.00	£10.00

The average pub or café price for drinks is:

coffee	60p	spirits (1 measure)	95p
tea	45p	beer (half pint)	70p
soft drinks	70p	glass of wine	£1

An evening out

The cost of this will vary according to area, cities generally being more expensive than country areas, although of course the range of places and prices is far greater:

cinema	£3.50 to £6.00
theatre	£8.00 to £27.50
concert	£5.00 to £25.00

Student reductions are often available if you have a recognized student identity card. The representatives of the National Union of Students (NUS) at your college will let you know where and when you can get reduced-price tickets. (More information about the NUS is given in Chapter 4.) Places providing music to dance to usually charge an entrance fee of several pounds and may also charge considerably more than pubs for drinks.

Travel

If at all possible, do allow yourself some money to travel, both within Britain and in Europe. Public transport in Britain is covered in more detail in Chapter 3 where you can find sample costs.

Coach and rail travel in Europe is roughly in line with the UK and again student discounts or special rates are usually available. If you wish to return home for a visit during your course, remember to allow for return fares home as well.

THE AU PAIR ALTERNATIVE

Single girls between 17 and 27 years of age inclusive with no dependants, who are nationals of a West European country (including Malta, Cyprus and Turkey) may come to Britain as au pairs, to learn English while living as a member of an English-speaking family for up to two years. This generally involves helping the family, for example, with the children, in return for free food and accommodation, a small amount of pocket money, and sufficient free time to follow a course of study. More information on au pair arrangements is available from your nearest British Embassy/Consulate or British Council office. If you visit Britain under this arrangement, bring with you, when you arrive, a letter from the family where you will be staying, with details of the family, the duties they would like you to carry out and the pocket money and time off you expect to receive.

BRINGING THE FAMILY?

Married students have the difficult choice of whether or not to bring their partners and children to Britain with them. You may feel you would like their company and that their presence would positively help you to enjoy Britain and study well. You may wish them to experience life here, or you may simply not like leaving them at home.

Some married students have thoroughly enjoyed bringing their families to Britain while for others the experience has been a disaster. The factor which seems to decide success or failure is the amount of planning and preparation put in *before* the family actually arrives. Families who come to Britain together, unprepared and 'hoping for the best' may be overwhelmed by difficulties. Those whose families join them later, when doubts about accommodation and money have been resolved, are likely to have a much more satisfactory time in Britain.

The information given below should help you decide whether to bring your family and gives some guidance on the planning and preparation you will need to undertake.

Immigration and employment

The dependants of EC nationals are usually automatically allowed to enter Britain for six months. However, there is a condition that they will not become a charge on public funds; so students will need to show not only that they can meet the costs of their courses and maintain themselves, but also that they can support their dependants. However, all EC nationals are free to take up employment or set up in business, without a work permit, so once in Britain the non-studying partner may be able to find work and contribute some earned income towards family funds.

Similarly, the wife and children of foreign or Commonwealth students will be allowed to enter Britain as dependants for the same period as the student husband providing the student can show he is able and willing to support and accommodate his wife and children under eighteen years of age, without the need for public funds. The wife will be free to get a job without Department of Employment permission but only if her husband has simply a student restriction from working. If the husband is prohibited from working here, the prohibition extends to the wife. Both husband and wife may also have to register at a police station if a note in their passport requires it (see page 33).

Husbands

As stated above, the wife and children of a male student have a right to join him in Britain so long as he proves he can accommodate and maintain them, and the whole family intends to return home at the end of his studies. However, the husband and children of a female student have no such automatic rights. It is more usual for the husband and children to be allowed into Britain only as visitors of the female student, not as her dependants. Visitor's status is usually for six months in the first instance, up to a maximum of twelve months. This also means that visiting husbands and children of female students do not share her National Health Service status and would require private medical insurance (see page 42).

Accommodation

This will probably be your major difficulty. There may be some married student accommodation provided by your college but you have to be quick off the mark to get it. It is usually heavily over-subscribed and often booked up before the end of the previous academic year. Similarly, some voluntary organizations have housing to rent but the demand for this, too, is great.

It is more likely that you will find yourself competing in the open market for private-sector rented accommodation. As there is a general shortage of family housing all over Britain, it may take you some time to find somewhere suitable at a price you can afford.

However, if you travel well in advance of your family, allowing yourself, say, two or three, or even up to six months to look for somewhere to live, you may be successful. You will also avoid running up huge hotel bills — a double room in a very modest hotel costs about £60 per day.

Chapter 4 covers types of accommodation and you may find it useful to have a quick look at it now. You will need the most expensive category of housing detailed in the chart at the end of the section of types of accommodation, so expect at least £156 per week in London and in the regions from £90 per week *and* all the other costs associated with renting a house or flat. Also, read the paragraphs on self-contained flats/houses, rent agreements, deposits and notice periods. Your tenancy will probably be for at least six months, so you will be committed for at least this period.

Children's needs

Naturally, couples will want to keep their children with them. But apart from needing more space and more money for living costs and return fares, there are several other practical considerations.

If the children are young you will probably have to look after them yourselves as domestic help is hard to find and expensive. There are private day nurseries which take children under school age, but many have waiting lists and the cost may be as much as £40 per week for each child. An alternative is a child-minder who looks after other people's children in her own home. The cost is from £35 to £40 and above per week. A list of registered child-minders is available from the Social Services Department of any local authority. Local authorities and a few colleges also run day nurseries but this is not a useful option as their waiting lists are too long. If the children are of school age (from five to sixteen years) and your course will keep you here six months or longer, you should be able to find a school to take them. But the local authority may not have vacancies. Also, to take them to school and collect them each day and look after them in the holidays may be difficult if one parent is in full-time work. Under British law, children under sixteen are not allowed to be left alone in a house for any length of time, so an older child cannot be left to look after younger children. Depending on how long you are in Britain, you may consider it is less disruptive and problematic to leave them at home with relatives.

Educational opportunities

It is almost as important for your partner to speak good English as it is for you. Everyday activities such as shopping and perhaps more important, making friends, will be very difficult with poor English, while getting work will be almost impossible. The effect can be very isolating. If your partner is willing to learn or improve his/her English, it shouldn't be difficult to find a course (see the suggestions on pages 7 and 74).

Once proficient in English, there are many part-time and evening classes on offer so that your partner, too, can take advantage of Britain's educational opportunities (for more information on these, see Chapter 8).

Counting the cost

You can work out most of the extra costs involved in keeping your family here from the information given earlier in this chapter and in Chart C (page 37) and Chart D (page 51).

The basic living costs for twelve months for a couple would be approximately £11,851 to £12,779. If you have children add a further £1,744 for each child. On top of these basic costs you may need to add a sum for warm clothing for yourself and your family, an amount for leisure expenditure and, possibly, medical insurance (see page 42). All this will be in addition to the costs of your course.

Supplementing your income

Please don't expect to earn any money by working if you are on a full-time course. You will need to satisfy the entry clearance officer that you have sufficient income without relying on part-time or vacation employment. The demands of the course are normally too great to allow full-time work. However, bona fide Commonwealth citizens and foreign nationals who are full-time students may work part-time for a maximum of 20 hours per week or in vacations, providing that their conditions of entry do not prohibit it and they get permission from the local Jobcentre (form OSS1). Permission maybe granted provided that:

- work does not interfere with study;
- no suitable British resident is available for the job;
- the student receives the standard rate of pay.

Vacation work can be a rich experience in itself by bringing you into contact with people outside your normal academic circle. However, it would be unwise to expect to make a lot of money. The student from Nigeria whom we quoted earlier found that vacation work helped him through his immediate financial difficulties and he enjoyed it as well.

> 'An idea came to mind – to go on a fruit-picking holiday camp in Cambridgeshire during summer vacation... Life in the camp was extremely lively. Camp is not only for British subjects. It was a camp for all nationals world-wide — West and East Europeans, Arabs, Africans even including South Africans and the Asian World. I made so many friends, male and female, many of them British, Italians, Spaniards and French... At the end of my holidaying – a little over three months, I made a profit of over £500.'
>
> Ajayi, F. 'Money makes the difference' in: *Overseas students — at home in Britain?* UKCOSA 1987

EC nationals do *not* need a work permit and may take any job (except in public service) without DE approval.

Having said this, the current high rate of unemployment in Britain means that not only are work permits difficult to get, but even EC nationals may not be able to find work. In Northern Ireland it is still more difficult for students to get permission, but if you want to try, apply to the Department of Economic

Development in Belfast (address in Appendix 2) and not the Department of Employment.

The wives of married students may be free to take employment without Department of Employment permission, depending on the stamp placed in the husband's passport on arrival.

SUMMARY — DECIDING TO COME

- *Standard of English* — make sure before you submit any applications for courses that your standard of English is good enough.
- *Costs involved* — find out as soon as you can exactly how much the tuition fees are at your chosen college; work out roughly what your basic living costs will be; don't forget to allow yourself a sum for entertainment and travel.
- *Bringing the family* — work out the additional costs involved; expect the hunt for suitable accommodation to be difficult and time-consuming; think about your children's needs; think about your partner's needs, e.g. language classes, work.
- *Supplementing income* — check whether your conditions of entry to Britain will allow it and remember, full-time work will be out of the question.

2
Making arrangements

Having decided that you want to study in Britain, the next step is to start making the practical arrangements. This chapter advises on the best order in which to do things.

CHOOSING A COURSE

The first thing to do is to choose and arrange your place on a course. Lists of further and higher education courses are given in the Education Information Service (EIS) sheets which you can get from any British Council office. Details of courses can also be found in the books listed in Appendix 4. After that you will probably want to consult individual college prospectuses.

There are colleges and universities all over Britain, each with its own areas of specialization. Once you have decided on the subject you want to study, it may be worth seeking advice from your local British Council office on college specializations, especially if the type of course you have chosen is available at a larger number of institutions. Also, it is worth noting that London colleges are no better and no worse than those in the so-called 'regions', and London living costs are amongst the highest in the country. City living in Britain is generally more expensive so if you prefer living in a smaller community you may have the advantage of paying less, too.

APPLYING

The demand for courses is always high with, as a rule, more people applying than there are places. So, to give your application its best chance, apply early. Most courses begin in the autumn (September/October) and you should begin making enquiries about eighteen months before the September you want to start.

Admission procedures

How to go about applying depends on both how you are to be financed and on what type of institution runs the course. If you have been awarded a scholarship, your sponsors will normally apply for you and send the written acceptance to you.

If you want to find out more about a course at a university, polytechnic, or other institution, write direct telling them what you have studied up to now. Admission procedures vary according to the type of institution you are applying to and to the type of course you wish to do.

First degrees

For first-degree courses at universities apply through the **Universities Central Council on Admissions (UCCA)**. This includes applications to Oxford or Cambridge but does *not* include the Open University, University of Buckingham and Cranfield Institute of Technology (Silsoe College, Royal Military College of Science). You should apply direct to these institutions.

Applications for admission to full-time undergraduate courses at polytechnics are made through the **Polytechnics Central Admissions System (PCAS)**. This does not apply to degree courses in Art and Design and those leading to initial teacher training B.Ed. (see below). For first-degree courses at colleges of higher education, apart from institutions included in the PCAS scheme, apply direct to the college. There is now a joint UCCA and PCAS form enabling candidates to apply for up to nine institutions.

Further education

Applications should generally be addressed direct to the institution concerned. Exceptions are as follows:

- To study **BTEC HND** at an institution covered by the PCAS scheme apply to PCAS.
- For **HND in Art and Design,** applications should go through the Art and Design Admissions Registry (ADAR). All other applications for HND should go direct to the institution.

Diplomas in Higher Education (Dip.H.E.)

Applications for a Dip.H.E. course at an institution in the PCAS scheme should be made to PCAS. In other cases apply direct to the institution.

ADMISSION PROCEDURES ACCORDING TO SUBJECT

Addresses of the organizations listed here can be found in Appendix 2.

Undergraduate level courses

- *Art and Design.* For university degrees, apply through UCCA. In the case of all other courses leading to qualifications in Art and Design apply either to Art and Design Admissions Registry or PCAS.

- *Nursing.* All applications, with the exception of degree and DipHE courses (UCCA/PCAS), should go to the Nurses Central Clearing House (NCCH). (See the paragraph below on Nursing training.)

- *Physiotherapy.* All applications should go through UCCA or PCAS or direct to the school if it is not part of either of these schemes.

- *Social work.* For all courses leading to the Certificate of Qualification in Social Work (CQSW), apply to the Clearing House for social work courses. You should first of all contact the Central Council for Education and Training in Social Work (CCETSW) for information and advice. For degrees, applications should go through UCCA and PCAS.

- *Teaching*. For first degree courses for universities and for colleges in the UCCA scheme apply through UCCA. For polytechnics and colleges in the PCAS scheme in England and Wales apply through PCAS. In Scotland and Northern Ireland apply direct to the institution.
- *Occupational Therapy*. All applications should go through UCCA or PCAS except colleges in Scotland or those not part of one of the schemes to whom you should apply direct.

Postgraduate-level courses

For postgraduate courses applications should generally be made direct to the individual institution. The exceptions are as follows:

- *Teacher training*. Postgraduate Certificate of Education (PGCE) applications should go to Graduate Teacher Training Registry.
- *Art and Design*. Apply through Art and Design Admissions Registry (ADAR).
- *Art education*. For specialist teacher training courses in this subject leading to Art Teachers Certificate/Diploma or relevant PGCE qualifications, applications should be sent to Clearing House for postgraduate courses in Art Education.
- *Social Work*. Apply through the Clearing House for Social Work courses.

Occasional students

To establish whether you might attend an institution for just one year or less as an occasional student you have to contact the institution direct.

For more details on these admission procedures and to obtain detailed addresses contact your local British Council office (or see addresses in Appendix 2).

Qualifications

The minimum entrance requirements for degree-level courses vary from one institution to another. However, they are usually two **Advanced Level General Certificates of Education** (GCE A-levels) and three different subjects at GCSE/GCE O-level. The BTEC National Diploma, the International Baccalaureate and the European Baccalaureate are also acceptable qualifications.

In 1988 **The General Certificate of Secondary Education (GCSE)** replaced the GCE O-level and Certificate of Secondary Education (CSE) in England and Wales. Overseas students are still able to study for GCE O-level outside the United Kingdom and the qualification continues to be recognized by educational institutions in Britain. An **International GCSE (IGCSE)** is available to overseas students and consists of a two-year programme leading to an international certificate. The examination which has been developed by the

University of Cambridge Local Examinations Syndicate (UCLES) is held twice a year at centres outside the United Kingdom in June and November. The IGCSE is accepted for matriculation purposes as a preliminary requirement for entry to British institutions.

From June 1989 a new examination, the **Advanced Supplementary (AS) level** has been available in England and Wales. An AS level is regarded as half a GCE A-level, so two AS levels can be accepted as equivalent to one GCE A-level for entry to degree courses.

In Scotland university entrance is normally based on Higher Grade passes, and generally four or more are required. GCE A-levels are also accepted for entrance purposes. Two GCE A-levels would normally correspond to four Higher Grade passes.

Overseas school-leaving certificates may fulfil entry requirements to British institutions instead of GCSE/GCE passes, but not all of them do. If you want to apply on the basis of a qualification from your own country, check first with the college you want to attend or your nearest British Council offices, whether your qualifications match the British requirement. If not, you may need to take a GCE A-level course, in addition to your existing qualification. It may also be possible to take a degree through a 'bridging' programme. For more details, look up the directories listed in Appendix 4.

Holding the minimum qualifications for entrance, however, does not mean a university or college will automatically offer you a place. The number of qualified applicants always exceeds the number of places available and it is up to the university or college to decide whom to accept.

Nursing training

Information on nursing training in their respective countries is available from the National Boards of Nursing, Midwifery & Health Visiting for England, Wales, Scotland and Northern Ireland (addresses in Appendix 2).

Applications for basic (pre-registration) nursing courses in England must be made through the English National Board Nurses' Central Clearing House (ENB NCCH) (address in Appendix 2). Similarly applications for courses in Scotland must be made through the National Board for Scotland Centralised Application to Nurse Training Clearing House (NBS CATCH) (address in Appendix 2). For Wales and Northern Ireland you apply direct to the insitution where the course is being held. The minimum age limit for entry is 17½ years, and the minimum entry requirements are five subjects at A, B or C grade at GCE O-Level, GCSE or International GCSE, or qualifications recognised as equivalent by the United Kingdom Central Council for Nursing, Midwifery and Health Visiting (UKCC).

In order to do any form of post-basic (post-registration) nursing training in Britain, an overseas nurse must first register with UKCC. To apply for registration you should write to the UKCC's overseas registration division (address in Appendix 2). In many cases, before registration can be granted, the UKCC will require the candidate to undergo a period of 3-12 months of supervised experience in the UK for which a fee may be charged. For certain post-basic courses temporary registration with the UKCC can be arranged. In these cases the need for adaptation training is not necessary. Information on post-basic courses can be obtained from the relevant National Board.

For both basic and post-basic nursing training candidates will normally be required to attend an interview. An invitation for an interview does not guarantee the offer of a training place. Overseas candidates may also be required to provide evidence of their English language ability.

Nursing training differs around the world and not all countries recognize British nursing qualifications. Before taking any decision about applying you are advised to write to the local nursing organization which represents your country on the National Council of Nurses.

COLLEGE ACCOMMODATION

Demand for college accommodation is always very high and when you apply for a course you should also ask for advice on living arrangements. Universities, polytechnics and colleges employ accommodation officers to help students, especially as first-year students are sometimes required to live in approved accommodation. Students whose programmes are administered by the British Council or other scholarship holders should apply for accommodation as soon as acceptance on a course has been confirmed.

If you are applying as a private individual, universities usually provide residential colleges, halls of residence, houses for small communities of single students and flats for married students but all this accommodation is booked up very early and first-year students are usually given priority. Colleges also usually have a certain amount of their own accommodation but, again, it fills up very quickly. As with the universities, as soon as you are offered a place apply direct to the accommodation officer.

DOCUMENTS NEEDED TO ENTER THE COUNTRY

The next step is to make sure you have all the right documentation to get through **Immigration**. Everyone entering Britain has to produce a valid international passport or equivalent document which satisfactorily establishes identity and nationality. Chart B at the end of this section gives a summary of the necessary documents but check with your nearest British representative.

Before applying for the relevant documents, there are two points you might like to consider first: your name and your date of birth. Problems often occur for students whose language has a different written script, or from countries where the way of recording names and dates of birth differs from British practice. It will avoid misunderstandings later if you decide on one way of recording your name and date of birth on all documents, for example:

- How do you want your name spelt in English? It is probably best to use the spelling in your passport. Decide on one spelling and stick to it.
- Which would you like to be used as your **first name** (forenames) and which your **family name** (surname)?
- Which part of your surname (if it has more than one part) determines its position in an alphabetical list? If Al or El is part of it, this is usually treated

as joined, even if your surname is not hyphenated.
- Some countries record only the year of birth, not the day and month, but you will find an exact date useful in the UK especially for driving, insurance and course application forms. So try and establish a definite date with the help of your family before you come and use no other.

European Community nationals

A valid passport or national identity card normally* entitles you to automatic entry into the UK for an initial period of six months and no employment restrictions are imposed. You do not need a visa or Home Office letter of consent, nor will you need to produce evidence of your acceptance on a course. But after six months you will need to apply for a long-term resident's permit (see 'Extending your stay', page 44).

Commonwealth nationals

Most Commonwealth nationals do not require visas but check with your nearest British official representative just in case you require one. In 1986, visa regulations were introduced for nationals of Bangladesh, Ghana, India, Nigeria and Pakistan, Sri Lanka and Uganda. Even if you do not require a visa you are strongly advised to obtain an entry certificate from your nearest British official representative, well in advance of leaving for Britain. This is not obligatory but it does make getting permission to enter Britain from the Immigration Officer on arrival much easier. Also, in the unlikely event of your being refused leave to enter on arrival, it entitles you to immediate right of appeal to an independent adjudicator, in the same way as a visa. By applying for one in advance you can confirm your eligibility for admission to Britain. When you apply you will need to show proof that you have been accepted for a course of full-time study with a reputable organization, normally the original letter from the college offering you a place, attending not less than fifteen hours per week for the organized day-time study of a single subject or related subjects: part-time courses will not justify an entry certificate. You may also need evidence of previous academic achievements and the entry certificate officer will ask you about the subjects and length of your course and possibly about your work plans when you return home after your studies. Finally, you will need to be able to show evidence (for example, a bank reference or a letter from your sponsors in Britain) of your ability to meet the costs of your course, accommodation, and maintenance to support any dependants accompanying you, without working.

The last two items, evidence of study and of adequate financial arrangement, should also be produced, together with your entry certificate, for the Immigration Officer on arrival in Britain, who will grant you formal permission to enter.

*EC nationals can be refused entry on grounds of public order, public security, public health or if there is a reason to believe they will become a charge on public funds.

Other foreign nationals (and some Commonwealth nationals)

You may need a visa from your nearest British official representative. If you do not need a visa, the Home Office strongly recommends that you apply, again to your nearest British official representative, for a Home Office letter of consent. This, like the entry certificate, is not obligatory but has the same advantages (see previous paragraph, under Commonwealth nationals). Like Commonwealth nationals you will also need evidence of full-time study (see definition above) and financial support, to produce on arrival. Please note that whether you have a visa, entry certificate or Home Office letter of consent to enter Britain, the dates of these stamps become irrelevant on arrival. The stamp placed in your passport by the Immigration Officer on arrival is then the important one.

CHART B: SUMMARY OF DOCUMENTS NEEDED

Documents needed depending on country of origin	Passport	Visa	If no Visa needed	Evidence of good health	Evidence of study	Evidence of funds
EC Nationals up to six months' stay	✓ or national identity card	–	– (after six months, a long-term resident's permit)	–	–	possible
Commonwealth nationals	✓	possible	advise entry certificate	possible	✓	✓
Visa foreign nationals	✓	✓	–	possible	✓	✓
Non-visa foreign nationals	✓	–	advise Home Office letter of consent	possible	✓	✓
Student nurses		as above		medical certificate and X-rays rec-ommended	✓	✓

Notes: (1) EC nationals may also need a landing card.
(2) The cost of a visa or entry certificate is from £20 – 85 depending on the length of stay.

Student nurses

The same principles apply regarding visas, entry certificates and letters of consent. You will also need written evidence that you have been accepted for training by a hospital and it will help if you have medical evidence of your physical fitness, including a chest X-ray.

Provided you have the correct documents on arrival, you will be welcome to enter Britain as a student and stay for the period of your studies. (Students are, however, expected to return home when their course of study is completed.)

ADVANCE TRAVEL ARRANGEMENTS

Having secured a place on a course and obtained all your documentation, you can then, if travelling by air, book your flight. It is better to arrive in Britain during the week, rather than on a Saturday or Sunday when many shops, most banks and offices are closed. There are airports in all the main British cities and if you are travelling on a scheduled flight it is quicker and more convenient to book direct to your final destination. If you book a charter flight to London it is cheaper to make any onward journey from London by train or coach.

Baggage and insurance

When you buy your airline ticket ask about your free baggage allowance as paying for excess baggage can be very expensive. Most airlines allow 20kg plus hand baggage on tourist-class flights but some charter flights only allow 15kg and hand luggage.

Sea travellers will find the baggage allowance quite generous but try to restrict yourself to an amount you can handle yourself, if necessary, as British Rail allows only 50kg (second class) or 70kg (first class) free of charge and it is often difficult to find a porter at the airport, station or dock. Excess baggage costs £2 for 5kg or part of 5kg.

At the same time as you book your ticket you can usually arrange travel insurance to cover both you and your baggage. This is a wise investment.

Money for travelling

There is no British limit on the amount of money you can bring with you in sterling notes, foreign currency notes, travellers' cheques, bankers' drafts or letters of credit, but you may need the approval of **exchange control** in your country. You will need some sterling cash (say £50 or £75) when you arrive for immediate expenses such as airport-to-town fares, accommodation, meals and porters' tips. Travellers' cheques can be cashed at airports, bureaux de change and banks but very few places offer a 24-hour service.

Heathrow and Gatwick airports both have 24-hour banks, but most banks in Britain open only between 09.30 and 15.30 Monday to Friday. Although **bureaux de change** stay open longer, their services cost more. Don't carry more cash around with you than you need: bringing some travellers' cheques in small amounts (£10 or £20 notes) will help you from the security point of view. However, there is a slight disadvantage in that banks charge for every transaction so you may be wise to bring one or two larger amounts (£50 or £100 notes) as well. A description of British sterling currency is given in Chapter 4.

CLOTHING FOR TRAVELLING

The unpredictability of the British weather is a national joke and cause for complaint. However, temperatures are rarely extreme as the figures below show:

Averages of summer and winter temperatures over a thirty-year period

Town	Average summer	Average winter
Edinburgh	12.9°C	2.3°C
London	17.0°C	4.8°C
Manchester	15.1°C	3.0°C
Southampton	16.8°C	4.6°C

This Australian student writes about her thoughts on the subject:

> 'The weather is such a clichéd subject in Britain that I hesitate to bring it up at all. However, since it is largely perceived by Australians as constituting one of the major obstacles to living a normal and happy life in Britain, it surely deserves at least a mention. Personally, I feel that the weather factor is overrated, certainly from a student's point of view. It is true that the weather determines the scope and nature of one's outdoor activities and that surfing and snorkelling, for example, are often out of the question in Britain. On the other hand, the British weather is itself a novelty to an Australian who has never before been challenged to work out the difference between 'sleet' and 'frozen rain'. In fact, inclement weather can be seen as quite a boon to the student who is looking for some reason to stay indoors and do some work. I have noticed that the British students frequently seem more genuinely depressed by the weather than do the foreigners, who are waiting to see what it will do next.'
>
> Vasey, R. 'Coming to terms with history and heritage' in: *Overseas students — at home in Britain?* UKCOSA 1987

Summer (June to September) is usually warm though sometimes humid. **Winter** (October to March) is cold and frosty, with temperature often below zero centigrade and some snow in the later months. Rain is frequent throughout the year so always have a sweater and light raincoat in your luggage. If you arrive in winter you will probably want to be able to put on a warm coat or raincoat as soon as you arrive, particularly if you have come from a hot country, but you may find it cheaper to buy the rest of your warm clothes in Britain after you arrive (see Chapter 5). It's useful to remember that you will be warmer wearing several thinner layers of clothing rather than one or two thick layers.

ARRANGING TEMPORARY ACCOMMODATION IN ADVANCE

If you are going to pass through London on your way to somewhere else, or have not yet managed to arrange permanent accommodation, you may need somewhere temporary to stay. If you write at least six weeks in advance to the London Tourist Board & Convention Bureau, 26 Grosvenor Gardens, London SW1W 0DU, they can make a provisional booking on your behalf and will write to you about it. Once in London you can visit the Tourist Information Centre at Victoria railway station (open 08.00 to 20.00 every day, with slightly reduced hours in winter) and they will arrange a booking for you. There will be a £5 fee and a £12 returnable deposit. The Tourist Information Centre also has an office situated in the main concourse of the underground station at Heathrow — open 08.00 to 18.30 every day of the week with reduced opening hours in winter. If there is a British Tourist Authority office in your own country they may be able to help you in advance.

If you reserve hotel or permanent accommodation from a definite date but fail to arrive on time, you will lose your deposit if the accommodation has been held for you.

The British Council books temporary accommodation in London for their sponsored students and visitors. Various educational institutions around the country are 'buying in' to this service. If your institution is part of the British Council's 'Meet and Greet Scheme' they will be happy to assist you on arrival in the UK. Inform your institution of your arrival details and they will in turn inform the British Council that you require assistance.

OTHER PREPARATIONS

Find out as much as you can about Britain before you leave home. Chapters 4 to 8 and the reading list provide a starting point. If you have friends who have recently visited Britain, ask them to give you their impressions of the country and any practical hints. In some countries, the British Council offers introductory courses to Life in Britain which are very helpful. Bring a few photographs of your family, friends and neighbourhood, and maybe one or two other things to decorate your room or flat with when you first arrive. You will appreciate having them to look at. You may also want to pack a few small inexpensive items typical of your country, to give to new friends. However, no one will expect you to do this so do not feel obliged. Check with the British Embassy, High Commission or Consulate that you are not planning to bring anything that the Customs Officer might object to; for example, there are very strict regulations on the amounts of alcohol, tobacco, perfume, etc. that you can bring in.

SUMMARY — MAKING ARRANGEMENTS

- *Choosing a course* – consult as widely as possible on which college, in which part of Britain, will suit you best.
- *Applying* — apply as early as you can, making sure that you know exactly how

and where to apply and that you have all the necessary entrance requirements; apply for college accommodation as soon as you are offered a place.

- *Official documentation needed* — make sure you have a valid passport or equivalent; do you need a visa, entry certificate, or Home Office letter of consent? Make sure you have written confirmation of a place on a course and evidence of funding; do you need evidence of good health?

- *Advance travel arrangements* — try to book your flight (or make other arrangements) to arrive on a weekday; make sure you know what your baggage allowance is; travel insurance for yourself and your baggage is a wise investment; bring some sterling cash and travellers' cheques to meet immediate expenses; bring a sweater and a raincoat; make sure you have arranged temporary accommodation if you think you are going to need it.

- *Other preparations* — seek out as much information as you can about Britain before you leave; pack a few photographs and mementoes to remind you of home; make sure you know the British customs regulations before you leave.

3
Arriving in Britain

Your first experience of Britain will be a crowded airport or seaport building; Heathrow, especially, is one of the busiest airports in the world so don't be surprised if you have to join a queue. Airports and ports are usually well signposted, so follow the signs which apply to you. Staff at such places are trained to be friendly and helpful so do ask for help if you need it.

IMMIGRATION

Your first priority is to pass through the passport and immigration controls so that you can receive permission to enter Britain. A student from Sudan described his experience of entering Britain like this:

> 'It was about three o'clock in the afternoon. My heart was beating at a rate of about 120 per minute as I approached the Immigration Officer at Heathrow airport... The Immigration Officer was a young man with a beard and well-built body. I presented my immigration papers to him. He asked me questions softly and politely and I answered confidently, for by now my heart had slowed down.'
>
> Sereke, K. 'A story of a villager in London' in: *Overseas students — at home in Britain?* UKCOSA 1987

When you reach immigration control you should have all your documents ready (see Chart B in Chapter 2). When these have been checked, the Immigration Officer will stamp in your passport the initial length of time you can stay in Britain, which for most overseas students is a year at a time. Don't worry if you know you will need to stay longer than the stamp says; you can almost certainly get your stay extended and this can be organized later, when you have settled down (see page 44, Chapter 4). The Immigration Officer will also endorse your passport with any additional restrictions which apply to you. For example, students from outside the Commonwealth and EC may need to register with the police. This can be done when you reach your final destination (see page 33).

The Immigration Officer may also decide to send you for a routine health check. It is routine so don't worry about it, but it is important to remember, after seeing the airport doctor, to return to immigration control to have your passport stamped.

If any problems should arise at immigration control there are people who can help you. You can either ask to see a representative of the UK Immigrants Advisory Service (UKIAS) (address in Appendix 2) or ask the Immigration Officer to get in touch with your college welfare officer.

More information on these sources of help is given in the section 'Sources of help' on page 74.

Going through customs

After immigration you can go to the baggage reclaim area and collect your luggage which by now will have been unloaded. Next stop is the customs hall. You must check at the British Embassy, High Commission or Consulate before you leave home what you can and cannot bring into Britain and what you need to declare to the customs officer. In most airports and ports in Britain you will find two channels to pass through customs, one sign in red and one in green; the green channel is only for people who are sure they have no goods to declare; it is subject to spot-checks by a customs officer. You should go through the red channel as you will almost certainly be carrying some items to be declared. (Visitors arriving in cars can get red or green windscreen stickers on the boat and will then be directed how to drive through customs.) If requested you must open, unpack and repack your own luggage.

MAKING TELEPHONE CALLS

You may need to make telephone calls very soon after you arrive. There are usually clearly signposted public telephones at all main arrival points and stations, and in some large shops and public buildings such as post offices. In the street, the once familiar and easily recognizable red kiosks have virtually been replaced by American-style steel and glass booths with red, blue and grey British Telecom logos prominently displayed somewhere — usually on the glass doors or sides.

Public telephones are either coin-box operated or Phonecard operated and both types will be available at your arrival point. Instructions on how to use both types should be displayed clearly beside them but if these are not clear ask someone for help. For inland calls you will generally need 10p, 20p, 50p and £1 coins. A Phonecard entitles you to a specific number of units so your calls are paid for in advance. At ports and airports there will be a sign near the telephones telling you where you can buy one. Elsewhere they are readily available at a number of outlets including newsagents and main post offices.

There are also international telephone boxes in airports, ports, large railway stations and some main post offices. They display an 'International Calls' sign overhead and will only handle calls that can be dialled direct. In London you can also go to:

The Westminster International Telephone Bureau
1 Broadway
London SW1
(open 09.00 to 17.30)

If you are having trouble placing a call, dial 100 for the operator who can also tell you what to dial for the various information services, e.g. **directory enquiries**, which can find you almost any number in the country.

Post offices and public libraries hold telephone directories including the *Yellow Pages* which is the commercial and group services listing (doctors, shops, electricians, etc.). British Telecom, the company which runs the telephone service, also publishes a leaflet which details the charges on private telephones. Telephone calls, particularly long distance, can be expensive, so bear in mind if you use the telephone in someone's house how much you will be adding to their bill. Telephone calls made from hotels are charged at a much higher rate than those made from a call box.

SECURITY

In large cities and crowded places such as airports and stations, there is the risk of theft. To avoid the distress of losing important documents and valuables as soon as you arrive, here are some important do's and don'ts.

Money

DON'T carry more cash than you need for daily expenses. If you stay at a hotel DO ask the manager to keep large sums of cash, documents and valuables in the hotel safe and give you a receipt for them. This is a free service. If cash is stolen, it is very unlikely to be recovered. DO keep separately a note of the serial numbers on your travellers' cheques, so if they are lost you can inform your bank. DO take particular care of bank and credit cards.

Handbags and luggage

DO carry wallets and purses in an inside pocket or handbag. DON'T ever leave a bag unattended and make sure it is securely fastened when you are carrying it. DO carry jewellery and valuables such as cameras, radios, typewriters on you or with you and keep a note of any serial numbers.

Documents

DO take special care of your passport, travel tickets and other important documents; documents are at risk particularly at airports and stations where it is obvious that most people will be carrying them. DO make a note, and keep it in a safe place, of the number of your passport, its date and place of issue. This makes replacement easier if you are unlucky enough to lose it.

Left luggage and lost property offices

If you don't want to carry heavy luggage around with you, you can leave it in a 'left luggage office' at most large stations and pick it up later. Keep the receipt so that you can reclaim your luggage. Check the opening hours or you may find your luggage locked away when you need it again.

If you lose any of your luggage in transit, take this up immediately with the officials of the airline or shipping line, but don't worry too much; ninety-eight per cent is found within three days. If you lose anything at the airport or station, go first to the lost property office there, as it may have been found and handed in. If you lose luggage in the street, or suspect it has been stolen rather than gone astray, find the nearest policeman who will advise you what to do.

TRAVEL AND TRANSPORT

Travel to and around central London

If your visit to Britain has been arranged by the British Council, your local British Council office will advise you on what to do when you arrive. You may, however, also find it useful to read what follows:

London has two main airports — Gatwick and Heathrow. From Gatwick you can catch a mainline train direct to Victoria railway station or an express coach to Victoria coach station. From Heathrow you can get to central London by bus, for example you can take the **A1 Airbus** service to Victoria coach and railway stations, or the **A2** to Euston railway station; or go by **Underground** (also known as the tube) on the Piccadilly line. These services are the cheapest and easiest way to travel to central London. Taxis are much more expensive and it is not a good idea to take them from the airport to central London unless this is the only way you can handle your luggage. The approximate taxi fare from Heathrow airport to central London (Piccadilly) is £30–35. Once you are in central London the advantage of taking a taxi is that it can take you right to your door; however London covers an area of 610 square miles and your journey can still be expensive. Use only licensed taxicabs (large and usually black with a special Hackney Carriage licence number plate on the back). These cab drivers know London and can offer helpful advice. Ask them how much the fare is likely to be and check you have enough English money to cover it. When you arrive, the fare will be shown on the meter in front of the cab, plus the 'extras' or additional charges for extra passengers and large pieces of luggage. If there has been a recent increase in taxi fares, some meters may not yet have been adjusted to the new rates. In this case an 'additional fares list' is displayed inside the passenger section of the cab which converts the fare on the meter to the new rate. Taxi drivers will always expect a tip, usually about ten per cent, or more if they have helped to carry luggage and on short journeys. Average taxi prices outside London are about £1.10p per mile, higher in London. Taxi drivers also have the right to refuse to take you further than six miles (ten km) because they may find it difficult to find a returning passenger.

Cheaper alternative ways of travelling in and around London are to use the extensive bus and underground rail (tube) services, especially if you have taken advantage of the various saver and season tickets available. Details of these can be obtained from London Transport, 55 Broadway, London WC1 or the British Tourist Authority, 'Welcome to Britain' Tourist Office, 64 St. James's Street, London SW1A 1NF, or The British Travel Centre, 4-12 Regent Street, SW1 (south of Piccadilly Circus) London.

Travelling to and around other towns

Ask at the information desk at your point of arrival which is the best way to make your onward journey. If you are travelling by train from the South East of

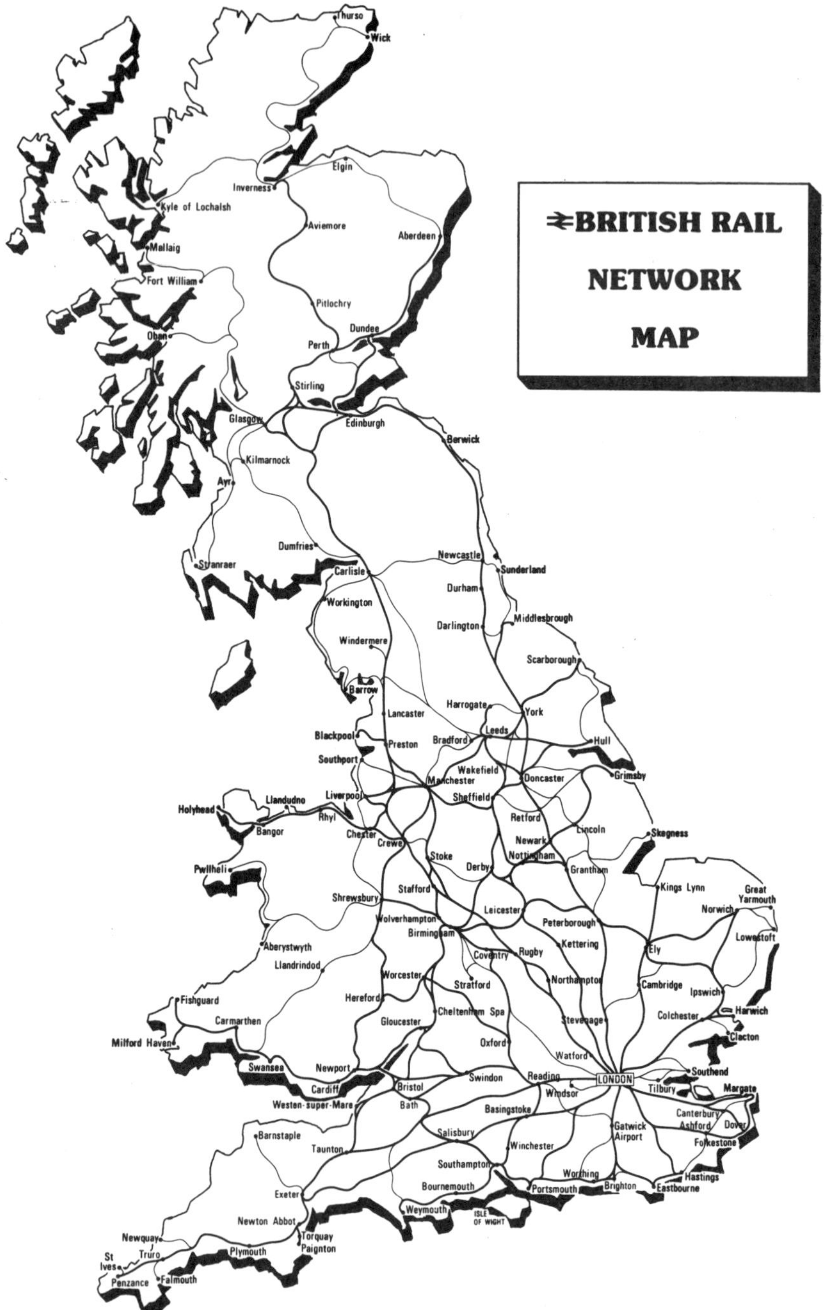

The main railway lines of Britain

England you will usually need to go into central London first but there are nine mainline British Rail stations around London from which trains leave for different parts of Britain. Ask which of these stations you need and how best to reach it.

British Rail express trains (generally known as InterCity) provide fast, frequent services between the major cities and towns. The coach services which operate from London's Victoria coach station are also good and cheaper, though slower, than travelling by rail. There is also a network of domestic air routes, but these are generally more expensive than rail travel although if you are prepared to go 'stand-by' (without advance booking) they can compare with the train fare. Most InterCity trains have buffet cars and there are 'sleepers' which can be booked at extra cost on overnight trains. You can also take a car on some trains — ask about the Motorail service.

There are two classes of fares on the train, the first-class fare being approximately fifty per cent more expensive than second class. There are often cheaper rates available for students or if you are prepared to go on certain trains. Once you have settled in, the NUS (address in Appendix 2) will advise you how to get your Student Railcard which entitles you to student rates from British Rail if available (34 per cent discount except on Apex tickets).

The following table illustrates differences in *return* fares by air, train and coach from London to Manchester:

Air	— stand-by	£130
	— full economy	£168
	— Apex	£ 88
British Rail	— normal first class	£125
	— normal standard class	£ 84
	— cheap (according to time and day of travel)	£ 33 to 43
	— Apex	£ 26
Coach	— normal	£ 23.50

Although taxi fares in the regions tend to be less than those in London, it is still much cheaper to get around by bus, and again season tickets are readily available. However, on first arrival, you would probably be wise to take a taxi from your final destination to your accommodation address and think about familiarizing yourself with the local transport arrangements later.

Nowhere in Britain has such an extensive underground rail network as London but smaller-scale systems exist and are well used in Liverpool, Glasgow, and Tyneside where it is incorporated into a rapid-transit system and 'light railway'. Such systems, which are designed to get people around metropolitan areas as efficiently as possible are also being introduced in other cities, such as Manchester.

REGISTERING WITH THE POLICE

When you reach your final destination, if your passport endorsement shows you need to register with the police, you should do so straightaway. This is routine procedure for anyone from outside the EC or Commonwealth. If you are not going to your final destination within seven days, you should register with the police in your first area and then transfer your registration when you reach your final destination.

If you are staying permanently in London, go to the Aliens' Registration Office (address in Appendix 2) and allow yourself time to wait in case there is a queue. If you are staying outside London, ask at your nearest police station for the address of the office with whom you should register. To register you need your passport, two recent passport-size black and white photographs and the registration fee (payable each time you apply for a registration certificate) which in May 1989 was £30. Do keep a separate note in a safe place of the number of your alien's registration certificate and its date and place of issue in case you are unlucky enough to lose it.

You must always inform the police within seven days of any change of address and of any extension of your permission to stay in Britain. You are required by law to carry with you your alien's registration certificate, but not your passport.

SUMMARY — ARRIVING IN BRITAIN

- *Immigration* — have all your documents ready; note what the Immigration Officer stamps in your passport; if sent for a routine health check remember to return to immigration control afterwards to get your passport stamped; don't be afraid to ask for help if you need it; if any problems arise at immigration control ask to see someone from the UK Immigrants Advisory Service or that your college welfare officer be contacted.
- *Customs* — go through the red goods-to-declare channel; you will almost certainly be carrying something that Customs will want to know about.
- *Telephone calls* — if you want to make a call soon after arrival either make sure you have a quantity of the correct coins or buy a Phonecard.
- *Security* — don't carry around large amounts of cash; take special care of documents, credit cards and valuables; note any serial numbers and the number of your passport.
- *Left luggage and lost property* — keep the receipt from the left luggage safely and check the opening hours; report any loss of luggage in transit immediately to the airline or shipping line, but don't worry, it usually turns up; for losses at the airport or railway station go to the lost property office; for losses elsewhere ask a policeman's advice.
- *Travel and transport* — avoid taking taxis if you possibly can; use the cheaper bus and underground alternatives; British Rail provides a network of fast, frequent services between the major cities and towns.
- *Registering with the police* — if your passport endorsement shows you need to register with the police, do so as soon as you reach your destination; keep a note of the number on the alien's registration certificate and its date and place of issue; carry it with you at all times.

4
Early days

When you have arrived in the town where you are going to study, and settled in your temporary or college accommodation, there will be many things you will want to do; acquaint yourself with the college, familiarize yourself with the town, sort out your finances, make health arrangements, etc.

PERMANENT ACCOMMODATION

However, if you have not been successful in obtaining college accommodation, your next step will be to think about finding somewhere more permanent to live. Be prepared for difficulties! There are still housing shortages in Britain; in particular furnished flats to rent at a reasonable price are hard to find, especially in cities and university towns. You will very likely end up living some distance from your college and spending anything up to an hour travelling to it.

Sources of help

As mentioned in Chapter 2, students whose programmes are administered by the British Council or other scholarship holders will be helped to find rooms. The British Council's Accommodation Unit (address in Appendix 1) may also be able to help you find long-term accommodation — that is, over four weeks, if you are a full-time private student studying in central London. You may visit the office between 09.00 and 16.00 Monday to Friday and must take documents confirming your course and financial status when you go. Universities, polytechnics and colleges employ accommodation officers who will also do what they can to help.

Try to arrive in Britain sufficiently early to allow yourself plenty of time to look, and be prepared to pay a higher rate for temporary accommodation whilst doing so. You will also find that you probably have to compromise between what you would ideally like and what you can afford.

TYPES OF ACCOMMODATION

Hostels

These provide rooms for both single and married students; some provide food and some have self-catering facilities. You should apply direct. There is a list of hostels and addresses in Appendix 3.

Lodgings

Sometimes known as 'digs', these are usually bed-sitting rooms in a private house. Rent is payable weekly, fortnightly or monthly to the landlord or landlady (who lives on the premises) and will include either breakfast or 'half-board' (breakfast and evening meal). Fewer private householders are offering lodgings now, but you can find out about them through the accommodation officer at your college or by watching the advertisements in local newspapers and newsagents or sub-post office windows. Boarding houses are houses where the owner regularly takes in several lodgers and may provide either half-board or cooking facilities.

Bedsitters

One room sharing kitchen and bathroom, these are usually rented out by private owners who advertise them in the same way as lodgings.

Self-contained furnished flats/houses

These are relatively scarce and comparatively expensive (houses more so) although of course they give you more freedom and independence. Usually you will have to sign a legal agreement or lease with the owner and the initial costs (e.g. deposit required) will be higher. Rented unfurnished flats are almost impossible to find.

Rent agreements

When you are looking at places to rent, make sure you find out exactly what is covered by the rent. Does it cover some meals, heating and lighting, hot water, use of a telephone or TV? In lodgings, bedsitters and some flats, gas and electricity may be metered, which means you have to pay for it by putting coins in a meter.

Your landlord or landlady will usually expect the rent on a fixed day, weekly or monthly in advance. If rent is paid in cash it would be sensible to ask for a rent book. A rent book may also list certain 'house rules' (or these may be displayed elsewhere in the house). Check you understand these and can keep to them as they may form part of your contract of tenancy and are usually aimed at keeping the household running cheerfully and smoothly.

In self-contained flats, your rent will usually be paid monthly and your landlord or landlady is unlikely to live on the premises. Any rules you are required to keep will be laid down in the lease or agreement you have signed which is legally binding.The lease will usually be for a specific period — for example six months, nine months or a year — and once you sign it you are committed to renting the flat for that length of time. So study the lease carefully before signing, and if necessary take legal advice. After signing, keep your copy in a safe place.

Deposits

You may be asked for a deposit in addition to rent in advance. The deposit should not be more than two months' rent. Ask exactly what it is for. For example, is it against damage (other than normal wear and tear), or instead of notice (in case you leave without giving the required amount of warning)? You ought to get a receipt for any deposit and this should state what it is for, and whether it is returnable when you leave.

Notice periods

If the lease is not for a specific period (for example six months, nine months or a year), generally speaking, the period of notice you are required to give when leaving a place is related to how often you pay your rent. If you have signed a lease, this will usually state the notice required on either side. If you have no written agreement, make a definite verbal arrangement at the beginning of the tenancy so that you know how much notice you will need to give and how much notice you will be given. Both tenants' and landlords' rights are laid down very clearly in the law so you will have a right of appeal if they do not keep their side of the bargain. If you have any problems over tenancy agreements, the **Citizens Advice Bureau** is the best place to go.

MONEY

At the same time as looking for somewhere to live you will probably want

CHART C: ACCOMMODATION CHART WITH AVERAGE PRICES

Types of accommodation	Food provided	Minimum price per week	
		London	regions
Residential colleges	breakfast and evening meal	£60	£38
Halls of residence Student hostels (usually single rooms offered to overseas students for the first year.)	lunch at weekends	£40	£30
Lodgings, boarding houses: single room	breakfast only	£62	£35
single room	breakfast, evening meal, lunch at weekends	£74	£60
Flatlets, bedsitters: single furnished room	own cooking facilities in shared kitchen	£55	£35
double furnished room		£83	£50
Furnished flats: small flats for two people	own cooking facilities	£136	£60
larger flats/houses for families with children	own cooking facilities	£156	£90

Note: If you share a double room, prices are a little less, but don't try to share a single room without the permission of your landlord/landlady.

to start organizing your finances. First, you will need to know about the currency. Britain's decimal currency is based on the pound sterling (£) which is divided into one hundred pence (100p). Coins are issued up to the value of £1. There are £5, £10, £20, £50 and £100 notes. You may also find some old silver coins marked two shillings and these correspond to ten pence pieces. Scottish and Northern Irish banks have their own notes which circulate along with Bank of England currency. Southern Irish money is foreign currency.

Banks

One of the safest places to keep your money is a bank; choose one that is near where you study.

All the major banks in Britain offer special facilities for students and will be only too happy to explain how to open an account. The most useful type of account is a current account. You can pay in money received in any form and then draw it out when you need it by using your cheque book. Payments to other people can be made by writing out cheques in their name. If you want to draw out cash for yourself, make the cheque payable in your own name or 'to cash'. A cheque **crossed** with two parallel vertical lines is even safer as it must be paid into a bank account. Payment by crossed cheque has the added advantage that when the person to whom you have given the cheque presents it at a bank, it will eventually come back to your bank and provide proof of payment. Most people now ask their bank to supply only ready-crossed cheques.

Most banks don't make charges if you keep more than a certain amount of money in your account. However, you shouldn't **overdraw** on your account (i.e. withdraw more money than you have in) without the bank's permission. If you borrow money from the bank there will be an interest charge. You will also have to pay a small charge to convert foreign currency paid into your bank into sterling.

If you have more money than you need for month-to-month expenses, it is a good idea to open a deposit account for some of it, where it can earn interest. This interest is taxable, but if your bank knows that you are not normally resident in Britain then you do not pay tax on it. You can't pay by cheque on a deposit account and to withdraw money you may have to give the bank seven days' notice or you lose seven days' interest.

When you have established yourself as a satisfactory customer with the bank, they can issue you with a cheque card. This is really an identity card which guarantees that correctly written cheques up to the value of £50 will be honoured by the bank. A cheque card is extremely useful as many shops and enterprises, particularly in London and the cities, will not accept a cheque unless it is backed by a cheque guarantee card.You can also use it with your cheque book to draw up to £50 cash from almost any bank in Britain. If you also ask for a Eurocheque card this can be used in the same way to draw cash from most banks in Europe.

Many banks provide dispensing machines, generally set in the wall of the bank outside, where you can draw cash when the bank is crowded or closed.

Provided you are a satisfactory customer the bank can issue you with a cash card for this purpose.

> 'My mouth was wide open in wonder when I saw a friend extracting money from a window in a wall.'
>
> Sereke, K. 'A story of a villager in London' in: *Overseas students — at home in Britain?* UKCOSA 1987

Building societies

Building societies in Britain were originally established to provide loans (mortgages) for house purchase/improvement to people who saved or invested in them. In 1987, however, the regulations governing institutions offering financial services to the public were relaxed. As a result, banks and building societies now compete directly with one another for customers. This has led to an increasing number of building societies offering current account services very similar to those provided by the banks and sometimes on quite favourable terms. For instance, some pay interest on current accounts and some do not charge fees as long as the account remains in credit or even within an agreed overdraft limit. Perhaps the wisest thing to do before making a decision about where to keep your money is to carry out a bit of research. Visit a few banks and building societies to find out which can provide the best service for you and bear in mind that, if you eventually decide you have made a bad choice, you can quite easily transfer an account to a different branch of either a bank or building society, or close an account completely.

Insurance

You can find out about insurance from insurance firms or brokers, banks, or, better still, from the students' union office at your college, as there are often special student schemes which are less expensive. You should consider:

- Personal property insurance — which covers the contents of your accommodation which belong to you, and your personal effects;
- Personal accident insurance;
- Medical insurance — essential in some cases (see page 42);
- Check your bicycle is covered if you use one, and if you drive a car, motor insurance is a legal requirement (see page 48).

HEALTH CARE

Another important area to concern yourself with soon after arrival is the range of health care services available and how to use them. If you are on an award administered by the British Council your programme officer can advise on what facilities are available but you might still be interested in reading this section.

Britain has a National Health Service (NHS) which is financed and run by the Government. Treatment under the NHS is free to permanent residents in Britain, and most accident, emergency and community services (not including hospitalization) are free to everyone.

If you are on a course longer than six months, or if you come from the EC or from a country which has a reciprocal health agreement with Britain*, you should be eligible to free treatment under the NHS. Once they have registered with a doctor, your dependants, but not family members with 'visitor' status, will also be able to get treatment for illnesses which arise here, but anyone who comes with the specific aim of having treatment whilst here may have to pay for private treatment.

Those relatives or friends who visit you as 'visitors' for up to six months in Britain during your studies will not be considered as your dependants: you will need to take out private medical insurance for their stay (see page 42). Medical treatment is free except for a flat-rate charge towards the cost of each medicine; treatment by a dentist or examination or prescription by an optician have standard charges.

Registering with a doctor

For treatment under the NHS you should always go to your doctor first, except in an emergency when you should go straight to the casualty department of a hospital or telephone an ambulance (see Chart E, page 74).

If you are eligible for free NHS treatment, you are also entitled to register with a doctor. You and your dependants are entitled to register with a doctor only if you are registered on a course which lasts more than six months, although this restriction is lifted if you are from the EC or from a country with a reciprocal health agreement.

Everyone entitled to register should do so as soon as possible after arrival: please don't wait until you are ill. Lists of doctors who belong to the NHS are available from: the local Family Practitioner Committee (FPC); the local Community Health Council (CHC); the Citizens Advice Bureau; main post offices and public libraries (addresses in the telephone directory).

In Scotland the organizations equivalent to the PFC and CHC are the

*In addition to EC countries the following have reciprocal health agreements with Britain:

Anguilla
Australia
Austria
British Virgin Islands
Bulgaria
Channel Islands
Czechoslovakia
Falkland Islands
Finland
Gibraltar
Greenland
Hong Kong
Hungary
Iceland
Isle of Main
Israel
Malta
Montserrat
New Zealand
Poland
Romania
St Helena
Sweden
Turks and Caicos Islands
Yugoslavia
Commonwealth of Independant States and any state formally part of the USSR.

Note: This list may change as new arrangements are negotiated local health board or local health council, and in Northern Ireland the Central Services Agency.

Doctors are sometimes referred to as GPs, which stands for general practitioners. The list will not tell you much about each doctor, so to find one you think will suit you, ask local people or tutors at your college, and choose one who is easy to reach when you are not feeling well. Your university or college may have its own student health service, which may be the most convenient and useful place to go.

Once you have decided on a doctor, visit the surgery and ask to be included on the list of NHS patients. If he or she is able to accept you, fill in an application and return it immediately to the doctor or receptionist. In due course, you will be sent your medical or NHS card which will have your NHS number on it. Keep this safe as you will need to be able to produce it or the number when using other parts of the NHS.

If you have difficulty finding a doctor who can accept you (this happens to permanent residents sometimes too, in certain areas) the local Family Practitioner Committee is obliged to help you find one.

Once you have a doctor let the warden of your hostel, landlady or landlord know his/her name, address and telephone number. We hope the need will not arise, but if you are ill, please remember to let your college know.

Visiting your doctor

Surgery hours vary but there is usually a morning and/or an early evening surgery on weekdays. Many doctors operate an appointments system, so you have to telephone in advance and make an appointment to see them, or when the surgery is closed you can ring the emergency number.

Whatever kind of treatment you think you need, visit your GP first and he/she will refer you to a hospital for specialist treatment, blood tests, X-rays, etc., if these are necessary. If you are referred to a hospital, it is up to them to decide whether the treatment can be provided under the NHS.

Most doctors have extremely busy practices so unless you really feel too ill to travel, you will be expected to visit the surgery in person. If you are too ill, telephone or ask someone else to, describe your symptoms and ask for a visit. If you ring as early as possible in the morning, it is easier for the doctor to fit you in when planning the daily round of visits.

Your doctor will also prescribe any medicines you need. Take the prescription to the nearest chemist or, after normal shop hours, ask the doctor's receptionist for the nearest late-opening chemist. Unlike many countries, few drugs are available over the counter without a doctor's prescription. Each item prescribed is charged at the prescription cost rate which at the time of press is £3.75.

Women's health

Contraception and birth control advice are available free to women staying over six months or who come from the EC or a country with a reciprocal health agreement with Britain. You can either go to your own doctor or to your local NHS Family Planning Clinic.

If you should become pregnant, don't be afraid to go for advice to your doctor, a Family Planning Clinic or your college; there will be plenty of help and support available while you decide what to do. If you are unmarried you will receive exactly the same sort of advice and help as a married woman.

Advice on contraception, pregnancy and abortion can also be obtained from some private agencies registered with the Department of Health such as the Pregnancy Advisory Service and British Pregnancy Advisory Service (see address list in Appendix 2). Some local health authorities have set up Well Woman Clinics to specialize in all kinds of women's health problems. If you want to know whether there is one in your area, contact your local library, health clinic or doctor as they are often not listed in the telephone directory.

Dentists

You don't need to register with a dentist, but if you are registered with a GP for medical treatment, find a dentist practising in the NHS (your main post office will have a list) and when you ring for an appointment, ask if treatment under the NHS is possible, quoting your NHS number. There is no longer a flat-rate charge for dental treatment under the NHS, but patients will pay up to a maximum of £225 depending on the extent of the treatment required. Don't expect to be able to see a dentist straightaway; they are usually heavily booked up though they will try and fit you in if you are in pain.

Opticians

If you feel your eyes need testing, or your doctor suggests it, you may go to any optician for an eye test. The test will cost about £15 depending on the optician. Lenses and frames for spectacles are charged separately and can cost as little as £35 or over £100 depending on your choice.

Private treatment and medical insurance

If you are not entitled to register with a doctor under the NHS, you will have to pay as a private patient for each visit and the full cost of all medicines prescribed. If you are a British Council student you should check whether your sponsors agree to meet the cost of medical treatment for an emergency condition or whether you should take out medical insurance. Some NHS doctors take private patients and most dentists will. Private doctors and dentists will also be listed in the *Yellow Pages* telephone directory for your area.

Even if you are here for less than six months you will not be charged for immediate treatment at hospital casualty departments or for the treatment of certain communicable diseases which confine you to hospital. However, if you have to be admitted to hospital after an accident or in an emergency, or if you need to return for further treatment, you will be charged for this. Private medical treatment is very expensive and the cost of operations and hospitalization can run into thousands of pounds. So please take out medical insurance straightaway, to cover yourself. Of course, if you can arrange satisfactory health insurance before leaving home it is best to do so. There is no insurance cover for the cost of pregnancy or delivery of a baby for students here for less than six months or for the wife of a student.

INTRODUCTION TO COLLEGE LIFE

Having sorted out the most important practical arrangements, you can then start adjusting to college life. You will be sent **joining instructions** when the college you have chosen receives confirmation that you intend to take up their offer of a place. These will tell you about **registration** and **enrolment** on your first day (what to do and when). They may also include details of an orientation programme of events organized during your first or **freshers'** week. Alternatively, this programme will be waiting for you on arrival along with information about your academic timetable.

Try not to miss this week as it is the time when people come to you offering advice and guidance rather than your having to go and seek them out. It is also the time when you start socializing and making new friends. During the week various functions will be organized, with the social side of things much in evidence, and all the college clubs and societies, some of them international, will be out in force trying to get you to join. Be careful though, only join as many as you can afford to, both in terms of time and money.

THE STUDENTS' UNION

Freshers' week is also the time when you will be introduced to the **students' union**. Nearly all universities, polytechnics and colleges have a students' union or students' representative council which is affiliated to the National Union of Students (NUS). All students are thus automatically members of NUS. At the local level the student union officers are elected by students and policy is debated and voted on at union general meetings. The union also represents students on college committees. At the national level NUS acts in the interests of all students and campaigns on major issues such as grants, accommodation, fees and awards for overseas students and many more. NUS has permanent full-time offices in London, Edinburgh and Swansea.

NUS services

The local student union also provides a wide range of services for its members, perhaps the most important of which is welfare and academic advice and information. It provides information on immigration regulations, vacation employment, fees, awards and much else; the student union welfare officer or overseas student officer is the best point of contact.

The union also plays a role in the college's social life. Many activities such as sports, drama and debating are organized by the union and the union building is often the focal point of the student community and may offer subsidized meals, a bar, and common room facilities such as newspapers, television and indoor games. It is a place to meet people to find out what is going on.

As mentioned earlier, the NUS also offers various price concessions to its members, on travel for instance, and you may also be able to buy certain goods cheaper through your union shop and get other discounts, for example on theatre tickets.

Other student organizations

You may like to contact your Embassy or High Commission during your early days to see if there is a students' union society for your country. Other overseas student societies also exist for all students, regardless of nationality.

Some cities have a body known as the **Conference** (or **Council) on Overseas Student Affairs (COSA)** or **International Societies,** which coordinate the work of all the voluntary students. Most COSAs and International Societies, or their member organizations, arrange social gatherings, outings, hospitality in private homes and run clubs.Their aim is to help overseas students to settle into the locality and make friends. The addresses of the COSAs are available through UKCOSA or you can find out about them through the British Council.

You will also find other organizations outside the union, based in the local community rather than the campus, for example local church groups. These are discussed in more detail in Chapter 8.

HOMESICKNESS

After the excitement of the freshers' week has worn off, it is very common for newly arrived students to become homesick and lonely. This is true not just for overseas students, but for British students, too. So remember, if it happens to you, you really are not alone. You will find that the photographs and mementoes you brought with you from home will help, and that you will learn to cope better with your feelings as your surroundings become more familiar, and as you make friends and you hear from home. Above all, try to maintain your perspective and remember that thousands of overseas students have been to Britain to study and were very successful. You will be too. There are people ready and able to help you cope with this and other problems at your place of study or in your community.

EXTENDING YOUR STAY

As soon as you are settled, check whether you need to stay in Britain longer than the time initially stamped in your passport. There is generally no problem in getting permission for an extension, as long as you allow sufficient time for your application to be dealt with. To apply for an extension, or to alter any of the other conditions of entry, you should write to the Under Secretary of State, Home Office, Immigration and Nationality Department, or go in person to one of the public enquiry offices in Croydon and in other towns (for addresses see Appendix 2). Immigration officials also visit some colleges to deal with applications on the spot. You can apply at any time, but if any expiry date is involved, you must write not later than one month before that date, as there is no appeal if your application arrives late and is refused.

When you write explain the reasons for your request and enclose:

- your passport (or if you are an EC national, your national identity card, landing document and two passport-sized photographs)

- your police registration certificate if you have one
- a letter from your college confirming you are enrolled for further full-time study
- proof that you can still pay for yourself, for example, a bank statement.

Your passport is valuable so send it from a post office either registered or recorded delivery so that you have a receipt for it.

If you are from the EC, you can stay in Britain for six months without formality but will need a long-stay residence permit to stay longer. These are normally given for twelve months.

Should you encounter any difficulties with the Home Office during your stay, there are three sources of specialist advice you can contact:

- your college welfare officer
- Joint Council for the Welfare of Immigrants (JCWI)
- UK Immigrants Advisory Service (UKIAS)

The addresses of the last two are in Appendix 2.

SUMMARY — EARLY DAYS

- *Permanent accommodation* — do you still need to find permanent accommodation? The British Council and/or college accommodation officer may be able to help; make sure you understand your rent agreement, what your deposit covers and what notice period is required; if you have any problems over tenancy agreements, go to the Citizens Advice Bureau.
- *Money matters* — familiarize yourself with the currency; open a bank account or building society account; consider and buy any insurance cover you need.
- *Health care* — if you are entitled to register with a doctor, do so as soon as possible after arrival — don't wait until you are ill; if you are entitled to NHS treatment make sure you find a dentist practising in the NHS —not all of them do; there are a number of special health-care services for women, so use them if you need to; if you are not entitled to NHS treatment make sure you take out medical insurance; private treatment is very expensive.
- *Introduction to college life* — make the most of freshers' week; only join as many clubs and societies as you can afford; use the services offered by the NUS and other student organizations.
- *Homesickness* — remember, this is a common, normal reaction and should gradually become easier for you to cope with – if not, ask for help.
- *Extending your stay* — check your passport to see if you need to apply to extend your stay; make sure you allow plenty of time for your application to be dealt with.

5
Living in Britain

This chapter covers what you need to know about the public services, services for the disabled visitor, use of motor vehicles, shops and shopping, and the other services you will find that help make living in Britain reasonably comfortable.

PUBLIC SERVICES

The post office

Post offices are usually open from 09.00 to 17.00 Monday to Friday, 09.00 to 12.00 on Saturday. Apart from the normal postal services, many of the things we are required to do by law are handled through the post office and it is a useful starting point for information. Here are some of the many services offered by main post offices (small sub-post offices do not offer all these services):

- *Postal service.* In Britain, you can buy stamps from many local and high street shops, such as grocers, stationers and newsagents, as well as your local post office. There are two postal rates for inland letters, **first class**, which should arrive the following day, and **second class** which could take several days longer.

  Letters can be posted at the post office or in the numerous red pillar boxes or letter boxes set in walls on the street, which show the collection times on the front, and sometimes have separate slots for the first class, second class and overseas mail. If you want to send valuables, money or documents through the post, use one of the special services.

- *Paying bills.* The post office offers a banking service called **National Giro**. If you have a Giro account, you can use it to pay bills. Even without a Giro account you can pay many bills for nationalized and local services, by cash or cheque, at the post office — for example telephone, water, electricity, gas.

- *Savings.* The post office runs the National Savings Bank which operates in a similar way to a deposit account at a bank. Other forms of savings which can be 'bought' at the post office are National Savings Certificates and Premium Savings Bonds.

- *Sending money.* An alternative to sending actual cash is to convert it into a safer form such as postal orders and overseas money orders. You can also cash these at the post office if you receive them from someone else. This does not apply to all countries, however, and you should check with your local post office.

- *Licences.* By law you need a licence for a television set (the money goes to finance BBC programmes), and for a car (road vehicle licence). You also need a driving licence to drive a car. The forms to apply for these and various other legal requirements are all available from post offices.

Public libraries

These are a very good source of information; most of the common reference books you might need are held and there are also leaflets and posters on local community activities. Public lending libraries are free to local residents and some have reading areas.

Citizens Advice Bureaux (CAB)

These offer an advice service for all types of personal and legal problems, plus information on all state services. They are a very good starting point as, if they cannot help directly, they will always know to whom you should be referred. The service is free and confidential.

Services for the disabled visitor

During the last few decades in Britain the general awareness of the special needs of disabled people has increased and efforts have been made to help them to do the same things in the same way as people who are not disabled. However, there is still room for improvement and the golden rule is to check before you set out to make sure the place you are heading for will be accessible to you.

Specifically, let your airline/hotel/railway office know about travelling arrangements in advance if you need help, and free porters or wheelchairs and access can be arranged for you. British Rail has facilities for wheelchair users and other passengers — including some coaches from which a seat can be removed to let you travel in a wheelchair. The bus and underground systems, though, are not accessible to wheelchairs.

For the past nineteen years it has been the law in Britain for new public buildings to be accessible to disabled people. Unfortunately, however, there is still a large number of old inaccessible buildings, so, once again, you would be wise to check before you leave that you will be able to get in.

If you are a disabled motorist you can obtain a disabled person's parking badge which entitles you to park free of charge at meters (and also for limited periods in streets with parking restrictions). Entitlement depends on the severity of your disability and how long you will be staying in Britain. The organizations mentioned below will be able to advise you on how to go about getting hold of a badge.

Many organizations exist to help and advise disabled people, but your best starting point is The Royal Association for Disability and Rehabilitation. You may also like to contact the National Bureau for Students with Disabilities (SKILL) and the Holiday Care Service (addresses in Appendix 2).

PRIVATE MOTOR VEHICLES

Cars

If you want to drive a car in Britain it must be registered, insured and taxed. You should complete the transfer of ownership on the registration document when you buy it and if it is not taxed get a vehicle road-tax licence application form from the post office. With the completed form, you will need to provide the registration document, the current insurance certificate and, if it is over three years old, a current Department of Transport test certificate of roadworthiness (£16.65) from a garage. (This certificate is commonly referred to as the MOT certificate from the days when the Department of Transport was called the Ministry of Transport.) You will also need the means to pay the road tax, currently £110 for a private car. If the car is taxed when you buy it, check the expiry date and also keep a note of your insurance and MOT certificate expiry dates as driving a car without the correct documents can carry heavy penalties. The tax disc must be clearly displayed in the car at all times. Cars are taxed for six or twelve months at a time.

Drivers

To drive any motor vehicle in Britain you must have a valid driving licence and insurance. The minimum age for a driving licence is seventeen for a car or motorcycle (sixteen for a moped, invalid carriage or certain other vehicles). During your first year your own overseas driving licence or International Driving Permit will qualify you to drive. If this expires during the year, to continue driving you must either renew it with your home authority, or apply for a British provisional licence. Either licence can then be used to sit the British driving test. If you come from an EC country or one of the countries listed below* you can exchange your existing full licence for a full British one as long as you apply within the first twelve months of taking up residency. Thereafter you would need to apply for a provisional driving licence and, as a learner driver, would be subject to provisional licence restrictions.

A learner driver must display the prescribed 'L' plates on any vehicle being driven and must be accompanied by a supervisor (with certain exceptions) who holds a full licence for that type of vehicle. A driving test for that group of vehicle must be passed before a full licence is granted. Learner motorcyclists of Group D cannot ride a motorcycle over 125cc or carry a pillion passenger unless that passenger holds a full licence for Group D vehicles. Details of full and provisional driving licences can be found in the leaflet 'What you need to know about driver licensing' (D100), available at most post offices.

You will need to read and know the British Highway Code (available from most bookshops) which summarises the traffic laws. (You will be examined on this when you take your test.) Most important, in Britain we drive on the left and overtake on the right!

It is compulsory for anyone on a moped or motorcycle to wear a regulation crash helmet and for both the front seat occupants in a car to wear seat belts,

* Australia, Austria, Barbados, British Virgin Islands, Cyprus (Republic of), Finland, Hong Kong, Japan, Kenya, New Zealand, Norway, Singapore, Sweden, Switzerland, Zimbabwe.

and, if fitted, they must be worn by rear seat occupants as well.

Drinking and driving

The laws about drinking and driving are very strict and are rigorously enforced. Unless you want to pay a hefty fine and/or spend part of your stay inside a British prison, under no circumstances drive a motor vehicle if you have been drinking.Take a taxi or public transport instead!

Motoring organizations

There are a number of motoring organizations in Britain which offer a range of services to the motorist including breakdown and recovery, insurance and route planning. The two best known organizations are the **Automobile Association (AA)** and the **Royal Automobile Club (RAC)**. They both charge a membership fee and make individual charges thereafter for the particular services you want to buy. Other companies exist, too, and you may find that NUS members get special rates at some.

SHOPPING AND SERVICES

Shops and shoppers

Most shops are closed on Sundays but open all day Monday to Saturday. Many towns and villages also have a half-day closing during the week from about 13.00 but they may stay open later on another evening.

There are one or two shopping customs in Britain which may differ from your practice at home. Bargaining is not customary in shops; customers are expected to pay the marked price for goods. The famous British queue applies particularly when shopping. You may not always see a queue but those waiting are expected to take their turn.

In self-service shops and street markets, remember to take your own shopping bag because many shops charge you for carrier bags. In self-service shops, however, always put the goods in the wire baskets provided by the shop first, then pay for them and transfer them to your own bag later. If you forget and put them straight into your own bag and/or leave without paying, you may be accused of 'shoplifting' which can lead to a police prosecution for theft. Unfortunately, this is a fairly common form of theft in some parts of Britain and many shops have electronic detection equipment and a tough policy on prosecution.

If you are buying expensive household goods you may like to consult *Which?* magazine in a public library. In this magazine the cost and quality of products from various manufacturers are compared.

Consumer rights

In recent years, Britain has developed a considerable body of law to protect consumers' rights. For example, shops must exchange faulty foods providing you can produce a receipt, so do keep receipts and guarantees, particularly for major purchases. If you feel you have not been treated fairly either by a shop or for any service which you feel has not been carried out satisfactorily, go to the nearest Citizens Advice Bureau, whose address will be in your local telephone directory and they will explain your rights in the situation and help you to get satisfaction.

Prices and payment

Napoleon I is said to have remarked over 150 years ago that the British were a nation of shopkeepers; today the variety of different shops is certainly an advantage. They range from the internationally known department stores to much cheaper local street markets. The student from Sudan noted:

> 'One of the things I did not expect to find here is the open-air market. Places like Wembley, Shepherds Bush, Camden, and Liverpool Street market are what we in the Sudan call 'the people's market'. The way people advertise their merchandise through demonstrations and the way they express themselves and influence customers is remarkable. They have great theatrical skill and it is possible to watch all this for free.'
> Sereke, K. 'A story of a villager in London' in: *Overseas students — at home in Britain?* UKCOSA 1987

Most areas have what used to be known as 'corner shops' for local residents which often keep longer hours than the high-street shops. Their slightly higher prices are usually compensated for by their convenience. There are also discount stores specializing, for example, in electrical goods, where you may find prices much lower than in the normal high-street shops. In general, supermarkets and street markets are the cheapest places to buy food. Street markets are particularly good for fresh fruit and vegetables and in many places they have a wide range of imported foreign foods which may remind you of home!

There are also 'convenience' goods which are already cooked, need little preparation and are useful for people in a hurry.

VAT or Value Added Tax is a government purchase tax of seventeen and a half per cent added to many goods and most services. Most prices include tax unless otherwise specified, but on large purchases it is wise to check. As an overseas visitor you might not have to pay VAT on some large purchases (but you might then have to pay tax in your own country). Most large stores will be able to advise you.

You can pay for goods by cash, by cheque on a British bank account with a bank guarantee card, or by sterling travellers' cheques, usually with no problem. If the shop displays a credit card sign, it will accept that particular credit card.

But be wary of running up bills or entering into credit agreements if you are over here only for a short while. Do check with your bank, college or other advisers before signing credit agreements as the 'small print' clauses may not be to your advantage and legal English is often difficult to understand.

Clothes

If you've come from a very different climate it may be cheaper to buy suitable clothes when you arrive here. A wide selection of ready-to-wear clothes is available but the best value will probably be in the 'chain-stores', groups of shops with a branch in almost every high street. A range of prices for good quality clothes in two leading chain stores in 1992 is given in Chart D as a rough guide.

As a cheaper alternative there are markets in most towns and cities on certain days of the week where clothing, particularly casual wear, can be purchased at reasonable prices.

CHART D: CLOTHES — PRICE GUIDE

WOMEN	Min.	Max.	MEN	Min.	Max.
Underwear – Bra	£4	£11	Underwear – vest	£5.50	£9.99
– pants	£2.50	£4.50	– pants	£2	£6.99
tights	£1.50	£3.50	socks	£2.99	£4.50
blouse	£15	£33	shirt	£12	£35
T-shirt (plain)	£6	£11	T-shirt (plain)	£6	£17
jeans/trousers	£16	£55	jeans	£18	£60
warm sweater	£24	£38	warm sweater	£22	£39
Warm skirt	£24	£38	warm trousers	£22	£39
shoes – heavy	£22	£38	shoes – heavy	£22	£40
– light/sports	£17	£28	– sport	£17	£60
winter coat	£88	£130	winter coat	£65	£110
winter jacket	£55	£90	winter jacket	£50	£70
raincoat	£40	£55	raincoat	£55	£80
light jacket	£33	£44	light jacket	£27	£50
umbrella	£7	£11	umbrella	£9	£13

If you prefer to continue wearing your own national style of clothes, do so, but you will probably still need a warm winter coat, one or two woollen sweaters and probably a raincoat (mac) or umbrella.

Dress in Britain, particularly in college, is mostly very informal. It will usually be made clear to you, when you are invited, if an occasion demands something more formal or smart, but if in doubt just ask.

Launderettes/dry-cleaning

Services readily available in most shopping streets will be very useful to you if you don't have a washing machine or drying facilities in your rooms or college. You can take your clothes to a **launderette** where you can use the large, commercial, coin-operated washing and drying machines, either yourself, or sometimes, for a small extra sum, an attendant will do the washing for you (this is called a **service wash**).

Heavier non-washing items can be dry-cleaned in the many high street dry-cleaners shops, some of which will also do repairs. Again, the cheaper alternative, if you have several similar garments to do at the same time, is the coin-operated dry-cleaning machine at the launderette.

Tipping

Tips are mentioned, where relevant, elsewhere in this book but the British Tourist Authority gives the following summary of customary practice. There are no fixed rules and the amount you give can reflect whether you feel you have received good or only average service.

- **Hotels**. Many hotel bills include a service charge, usually ten to twelve per cent, but in some larger hotels fifteen per cent. Where a service charge is not included, it is customary to divide ten to fifteen per cent of the bill among the staff who have given a good service.
- **Porterage**. 30p per suitcase.
- **Taxis**. Ten to fifteen per cent of the fare.
- **Hairdressers**. £1.00–1.50
- **Restaurants**. Ten to fifteen per cent of the bill if service charge is not included.
- **Theatres, cinemas and petrol stations**. Tips are not expected.

Electricity

The British electricity supply works on 240 volts/50 cycles, so make sure any equipment you bring from home can be used safely on this voltage or can be converted. Most modern British buildings are now equipped with sockets which take the modern thirteen-amp square-pin plugs. These are fused plugs. Items such as blankets, power tools, stereo equipment, clocks and lighting up to 700 watts should be fitted with a three-amp fuse (red). Most other heavier domestic equipment needs a thirteen-amp fuse (brown). Some equipment is also earthed, that is, fitted with a three-core wire of which the earth wire is connected to the middle pin in the plug. Britain has now adopted the standard European colour code for wiring; the brown lead is the live lead and should be connected to the fused side of the plug, the blue lead is neutral and the green and yellow lead is the earth. If you have old-fashioned wiring or sockets with round pins in your building, ask advice on the correct plugs and wiring to use, and make sure you don't overload the sockets or circuits with too many adaptors. Also be careful if you buy second-hand electrical goods; only buy those conforming to British safety standards.

Emergencies

There is a national emergency telephone number if you need the fire brigade, an ambulance or the police quickly. Dial 999 (free from both public and private telephones) and ask for whichever of the services you need. When the operator puts you through, give your name and address or directions to where the

A few years ago new colours were adopted for wiring and any new appliance purchased now should be connected as shown in the diagram.

That is:–

Green and Yellow wire (earth) to terminal marked E or ⏚
Brown wire (live) to terminal marked L.
Blue wire (neutral) to terminal marked N

However some older appliances may have flexes which use the old colour code and should therefore be connected:– Green (earth) to terminal marked E or ⏚. Red (live) to terminal marked L. Black (neutral) to terminal marked N.

The large earth pin of a 3 pin plug should always be connected to the green or green and yellow wire as this helps prevent you suffering a shock if an electrical fault develops in the appliance. Always make sure that there are no loose wires and that the cord grip is holding the flex firmly.

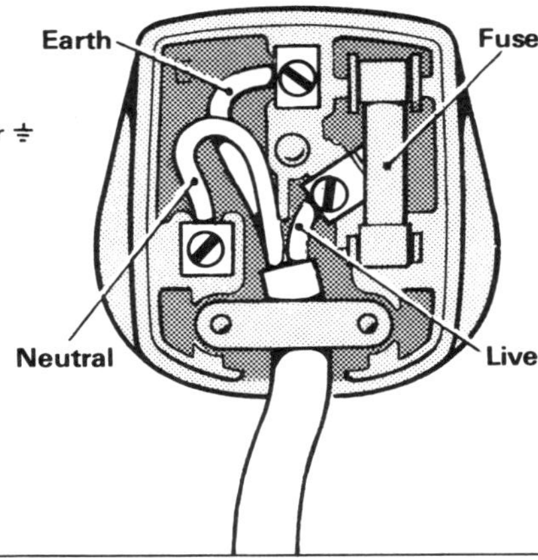

Some appliances are specially designed (double insulated) so that an earth wire is not necessary. These may use either the new or old colour coding system and the two wires should be connected accordingly. When connecting a 2 core flex to a 3 pin plug NEVER use the earth terminal.

IF YOU ARE IN ANY DOUBT WHATSOEVER CONSULT A QUALIFIED ELECTRICIAN.

Never use a 2 pin plug with a 3 core flex.

Always make sure you have the right length of flex on an appliance, (which normally should not exceed 2 metres, the exception being vacuum cleaners, lawn mowers etc.)

Never try to join two pieces of flex unless you have a proper connector.

Always use the right sort of fuse in your 3 pin plug.

Details of the British electrical plug.

Reproduced by kind permission of South Western Electricity

emergency is. You may also be asked for your telephone number.

Smoking

Smoking is less common in Britain now than it used to be and there is quite a strong anti-smoking movement. In many public places, such as shops and theatres, you may see no-smoking signs; cinemas often designate one side of the auditorium as a non-smoking area. Trains now have more non-smoking compartments so check carefully when you board one; there is now no smoking on London underground stations or trains. It should be noted that when seeking private accommodation you may find that in some cases non-smokers are preferred.

Where to go for help

Throughout this book sources of help have been mentioned under the relevant headings and Chart E at the end summarizes them for easy reference. The British Council can also advise you on most matters and Council offices are listed in Appendix 1.

SUMMARY — LIVING IN BRITAIN

- *Public services* — familiarize yourself with the range of services offered by the post office; public libraries are a good source of information on all sorts of things, they are free and some have reading areas; Citizens Advice Bureaux give advice on personal and legal problems and information on state services.
- *Private motor vehicles* — if you want to drive a motor vehicle in Britain it must be registered, insured, taxed, and, if over three years old, have an MOT test certificate; you must also have a valid driving licence; motorcyclists must wear crash helmets and front seat occupants in cars must wear seat belts; the drink driving laws are very strict, so don't do it; the AA and RAC are just two of the motoring organizations offering, amongst other things, breakdown and recovery services.
- *Shops and shopping* — there is a large range of shops, most of which are closed on Sundays; bargaining is not customary and you are expected to queue for service; never put goods into your own bag without paying for them, as most places have tough policies on 'shoplifting'; the Citizens Advice Bureau will be able to advise you on your consumer rights; consult the chart to get a rough idea of how much clothes cost.
- *Other services* — you will find launderettes and dry-cleaners in most shopping areas; there are no fixed rules on tipping but the British Tourist Authority has produced a useful guide on how much and when to tip for service; the electricity supply works on 240 volts/50 cycles so make sure any equipment you bring from home can be safely used on this voltage and that you are familiar with the fuse and wiring requirements — if in doubt, ask someone; the national emergency telephone number is 999 and it is free to dial it from public and private telephones.

6
People, politics and the law

In chapters 1 to 5 we have covered the practical aspects of studying and living in Britain. In this chapter, we move on to the more general areas of how the country works as a whole, the sort of people you are likely to meet and the kinds of attitudes you are likely to find.

THE COUNTRY

Britain, or the United Kingdom, is a relatively small group of islands made up of four distinct countries; England, Scotland, Wales and Northern Ireland. Although part of the same political and economic unit of the UK, each has its own distinct cultural identity.

Scotland

There are about five million people in Scotland, most of whom live in the southern central belt which takes in the cities of Glasgow and Edinburgh. In the north you find the 'Highlands and Islands' and this is where Gaelic, Scotland's Celtic language, is most widely spoken. Scotland has its own educational and legal systems.

Wales

Wales also has its own Celtic language, Welsh, which has undergone a revival in recent years and is now quite widely spoken. It also has its own Welsh-language TV channel and most road signs are in Welsh and English. However, most people in the larger cities and towns, like Cardiff and Swansea, and in the southern and eastern parts of the country generally, speak English either as their first or second language. So it is only in the far north or west that you might have difficulties making yourself understood in English.

Northern Ireland

Northern Ireland is separated from the rest of Britain by the Irish Sea. It is made up of six counties and although geographically part of the same land mass as Eire (Republic of Ireland or Southern Ireland), the two countries are politically and economically separate. The punt (Irish pound) is not for instance legal tender in the North just as sterling is not legal tender in the South, so if you are thinking of travelling between the North and South, you will need to change currencies. As a foreign national you will also need your passport to cross the border.

Northern Ireland, as you are probably aware, has its own special political problems. For this reason, the Northern Ireland (Emergency Provisions) Act and the Prevention of Terrorism Act apply to everyone entering and leaving the country. You may be asked to complete an information card by the police and it is an offence not to do so or to provide false information. At ports and airports you may also be asked to hand over your landing or embarkation cards. Also, you should be prepared to have your bags searched by security officers in public buildings and shops. This, however, is probably the limit to which the 'political situation' will affect you.

England

Within England you will soon become aware of different regional cultural identities. People in the North, for example, are often reputed to be more outward going and 'to say what they think' or 'speak their minds' more readily than those in the South. As with your own country, you will also find different regional accents, dialect words and colloquial expressions.

THE CITIES

London and the major cities are the most cosmopolitan areas of Britain and people originating from many countries are part of normal life. In more remote rural areas, people may still be less used to overseas visitors. However, cosmopolitan cities have their disadvantages. Life is far busier and noisier and people have less time to talk; the pace of life is faster; traffic is heavier and living costs are generally higher. Many people prefer to live outside the cities and 'commute' in to work each day. The buildings in some city centres have been taken over almost exclusively for commercial use and may be quite deserted at night when everyone has gone home. Despite this, people are still attracted towards the cities because of the variety of opportunity they offer; this goes some way to explaining some of the problems you may encounter in finding inexpensive housing.

THE PEOPLE

Britain has quite a cold climate for much of the year so social and family life is often centred indoors. Outside their homes the British tend to be reserved and there is little of the ease of falling into conversation that you find in hotter countries where much of life takes place outdoors, or even in European 'café' society where people meet, eat and discuss life in street cafés. Our Sudanese student comments again:

> 'The social life outside my surroundings was often disturbing. In the tubes, buses or other public places I did not see people speaking to each other. People often looked gloomy and seemed to live in their own world.'
>
> Sereke, K. 'A story of a villager in London' in: *Overseas students — at home in Britain?* UKCOSA 1987

However, when there is a hot summer in Britain, chairs and tables appear outside cafés and pubs, children play in the street, neighbours cluster round each others' front doors and the warmth seems to melt us a little.

British reserve is not necessarily unfriendliness, nor is it only foreigners who experience it. The British are equally reserved with each other as it is considered important to respect the privacy of others and impolite to intrude where you may not be wanted. It is frequently politeness which prevents the British from making the first move, but we can be very warm and friendly, though you must expect friendship to develop perhaps more gradually than you are used to at home.

ETHNIC AND NATIONAL MINORITIES

Many so called 'minority groups' have settled in Britain having left homes abroad for a variety of reasons – for example, to escape political or religious persecution. The largest such group is the Irish who left Ireland in the last century to escape famine.

In this century there have been refugees from Europe, many of them Jewish. The 1950s and '60s saw the arrival of West Indians and Asians, who came here to work. Then in the 1970s and '80s refugees from Uganda, Latin America, Vietnam and Sri Lanka came to live in Britain. Smaller groups of Americans, Australians and Europeans have also settled here. In some cases minority communities have chosen to stay together and keep their cultural traditions alive. In other cases, they have chosen to adopt a more 'British' way of life.

Unfortunately, despite this history and despite the fact that racial discrimination is against the law, you may still come across people who are racially prejudiced in Britain. If you do, try not to let their prejudice overshadow everything else and try not to let it force you into sticking solely with people of your own nationality, religion or language. You will probably miss out on a lot if you do. Prejudice in all things is usually the result of ignorance, so, the more you are able to meet and talk with people here, the more they can learn from you.

RELIGION

Although the state church in England is the (Anglican) Church of England and in Scotland the (Presbyterian) Church of Scotland, every major religion in the world is represented in Britain, a reflection of the variety of peoples and persuasions living here. As well as the many protestant denominations, the Roman Catholic and the Orthodox churches, most towns have a synagogue and most big cities have Islamic, Hindu, Sikh and Buddhist centres. If you have difficulty finding a place of worship, the students' union in your academic institution should be able to advise you.

Freedom of worship is a legal right in Britain and religion is regarded as highly personal: the British are generally reticent about enquiring into someone's religious views. If you belong to one of the well-known religions in Britain though, you may find British people genuinely interested in your religious customs and philosophy.

SEXUAL EQUALITY

British women, in common with women in most Western countries, have been fighting for sexual equality with men for much of the last century. Their achievements have been considerable. So, if you come from a society where women are treated differently from men, you will need to know what sexual equality means in Britain today.

First and foremost, under the terms of the Sex Discrimination Acts, discrimination against anyone on the grounds of their sex alone is illegal. For women, this means they are entitled to be accorded equal respect and status with men in all areas of life. This is why it is not at all unusual for women to go out and about on their own and to meet together in public places, such as cafés and bars, for business and social reasons.

Many British women expect to pursue careers for intellectual, financial and social reasons. They also expect, and are legally entitled to, equal pay with men for the same job. When they have family responsibilities, some women, depending on financial and other circumstances, choose not to work; others choose to take time off work while their children are young. In still other families, the father will give up work while the mother continues to pursue her career. In all of these cases, men and women are generally expected to share the domestic responsibilities at home with their partners.

POLITICS AND THE LAW

National politics

The British political system is rather unusual in combining monarchy with parliamentary democracy. In fact, the monarch, currently Queen Elizabeth II, has relatively little political power now, though she retains the title, Head of State, and plays a formal part in the political process. For example, the Queen opens each parliamentary session with a speech prepared for her, outlining the government's programme for legislation, and the Queen's signature is also necessary on all legislation.

Political power rests with the elected **government** (led by the Prime Minister and the Cabinet) based on the strength of their support in Parliament. For most of this century the government has been formed from one of three major parties: the **Labour** party, the **Conservative** or Tory Party, and the **Liberals**.

Coalition governments are rare in British political history, usually occurring only in wartime. Since 1945 governments have either been Labour or Conservative. In 1981 a new party, the **Social Democrats** (SDP), was formed but in 1988 the Liberals and most members of the SDP combined to form yet another party, the **Liberal Democrats**. There are also two nationalist parties — one in Wales (Plaid Cymru) and one in Scotland (The Scottish National Party), as well as a number of parties in Northern Ireland (the largest of these being the Ulster Unionist Party and the Democratic Unionist Party).

Parliament consists of two **chambers** or **Houses**: the House of Commons and the House of Lords. The House of Lords is made up of Lords Spiritual and Lords Temporal. Lords Spiritual comprises religious leaders, such as the Archbishops of Canterbury and York, the Bishops of London, Durham and Winchester and senior bishops. Lords Temporal are secular hereditary and life peers and peeresses of the United Kingdom. The Queen, acting on the advice of the Prime Minister, confers temporal peerages, usually in recognition of service to the country or to procure the talents and abilities of men and women whose advice is beneficial to the government but who do not wish to become Members of Parliament. This includes the Lords of Appeal or law lords who are created life peers to assist the House to carry out its judicial duties. However, it is the House of Commons, the elected chamber, which is the main area of British politics, the Lords being mainly a revising chamber.

The House of Commons consists of 650 full-time, salaried members each of whom represents a constituency, or particular geographical area. **Members of Parliament** (MPs) must put themselves forward for re-election at least once every five years when a general election is called. Hitherto the leader of whichever political party wins most seats (though not necessarily most votes) has been asked by the Queen to form a government. Within the five-year periods, elections can be called at the political convenience of the Prime Minister or if the government is no longer able to command majority support in the Commons. The largest minority party, currently Labour, becomes the official 'opposition' and has its own leader and 'shadow cabinet'.

Local government

In England and Wales the administration of local matters and services is handled by a variety of 'local authorities'. These have independent, locally elected councils with different responsibilities. For example, county councils are usually responsible for planning, roads and traffic, consumer protection, refuse disposal, the police and the fire service. Between them, the county and the district councils also administer education, libraries, the social services, environmental health, housing and the provision of museums, art galleries and parks. Local education authorities are normally responsible for administering and funding schools and further and higher education institutions in their area. (They do not fund universities, polytechnics, institutions offering mostly higher education courses or private institutions.) They administer the grants which 'home' students are given to take courses at higher education institutions. (In Scotland and Northern Ireland local government is run on broadly similar lines.)

Local government finance (until March 1993)

Everyone, with a few exceptions, aged eighteen or over, pays the personal Community Charge (or Poll Tax) in the area in which they have their sole or main residence. The average annual personal Community Charge for the current year is about £250.

The basic rules about liability to pay the Community Charge apply to full-time students in the same way as to other adults, although there are some special rules applying specifically to them. Your educational institution will be able to advise you further regarding registration for and payment of the Community Charge. Most full-time students will, however, have to pay only 20 per cent of the personal Community Charge. Spouses and children over eighteen will be required to pay 100 per cent of the Community Charge unless they are in full-time education. If your dependants are paying 100 per cent of the charge, they can apply for a rebate of up to 80 per cent. They will still have to pay some money towards it. You should note that Community Charge rebate is not a recourse to public funds.

The Council Tax (from April 1993)

From the 1 April 1993, the Community Charge or 'Poll Tax' will be replaced by a new system of financing local authority services. This new Council Tax will be based on the assessed market value of properties, and will vary from one local authority to another, and will be payable by most people over the age of eighteen.

Students living in halls of residence, student hostels, any other accommodation specifically provided for student occupation, as well as those living in privately rented accommodation where all the other residents are students, will be exempt from paying the tax. The regulations are more complex in situations where students and non-students share private accommodation. If your spouse joins you in the UK, she or he may be liable to pay the tax. At the time of going to press, no further information is available about how the tax will be administered or what the level of charges will be.

More information will be available from your place of study after April 1993.

The police

Britain's 51 police forces are divided on a regional basis and are each responsible for enforcing the law in their area. There is no split between political, civil or traffic police as there is in some countries. The functions of the police cover everything from protecting people and property (by patrolling in cars and on foot), through traffic control to crime prevention, investigation and the arrest of offenders. Police often become involved with social problems and can refer people to the various social agencies for help. Recently, more effort is being made in cities to improve police relations with local communities and to encourage members of ethnic minorities to join the police force. In general you should find the police polite and friendly. They are there to protect and help you, so don't be afraid to call on their help.

Traffic wardens (in black uniforms with yellow bands) come under the control of the police but their duties are confined to traffic and parking.

The law and citizens' rights

Broadly speaking, the individual is well protected by the law in Britain: for example, the laws to protect consumers or tenants and the laws against sex or racial discrimination. There is political and religious freedom and also the freedom of speech, an ancient right which Parliament has long upheld. The Sudanese student sums it up:

> 'The extent of freedom was unbelievable. Freedom of speech, freedom to criticize, to write and worship is something I have never experienced before. Political opposition leaders criticizing and joking about each other and yet never coming to blows is something I had not imagined possible.'
>
> Sereke, K. 'A story of a villager in London' in: *Overseas students — at home in Britain?* UKCOSA 1987

If someone is arrested, either immediately, or after a period of time, for some more serious alleged offences he or she is entitled to ask the police to notify one person (usually either a friend, relative or solicitor) and the police cannot hold anyone for more than a certain length of time without justifying their action before the court.

If you need legal advice, the best place to start is your local **Citizens Advice Bureau** (CAB). As well as advising you themselves, they can put you in touch with a **solicitor** (lawyer) and tell you whether you are entitled to free legal aid. Many cities also have free law centres, where there is at least one full-time qualified lawyer.

SUMMARY — PEOPLE, POLITICS AND THE LAW

- *The country* — Britain is made up of four distinct countries, England, Scotland, Wales and Northern Ireland and each has its own cultural identity; cities tend to be the most cosmopolitan areas of the country but the pace of life is faster, the traffic heavier and the cost of living generally higher.
- *The people* — tend to be a little reserved and friendships will probably take longer to develop than you may be used to; although racial discrimination is against the law, racial prejudice still exists; if you come up against it, you may wish to report it to the welfare officer at your place of study.
- *Religion* — every major religion in the world is represented in Britain; freedom of worship is a legal right.
- *Sexual equality* — sex discrimination is against the law and women are entitled to be accorded equal status and respect with men in all areas of life; don't be surprised if you see women socializing together or going out and about alone; men are generally expected to take an equal share of domestic responsibilities.
- *Politics and the law* — the national political system combines monarchy with parliamentary democracy; the administration of local matters and services is handled by 'local authorities'; there are 51 police forces and there is no split between political, civil or traffic police, their role covers everything from protecting people and property, through traffic control to crime prevention, investigation and arresting offenders; the individual is well protected by the laws in Britain; political and religious freedom and freedom of speech are fiercely defended.

7
Social customs

Every country has its own social customs; below is an outline of a few you will probably find useful to know about in Britain.

VISITING A BRITISH HOME

There is a commonly quoted saying in Britain, 'an Englishman's home is his castle', which sums up the importance we give to our own bit of private territory. Basically, if you are living in a British home or are invited to go and visit one, the golden rule is to 'act thoughtfully'. This means, for example, making sure that you are on time for meals or giving your host as much warning as possible if you have to miss one; checking whether it is convenient for you to have a bath, do your laundry, etc.; keeping your room clean and tidy; making sure you have a door key if you are going to be out late; letting your hosts know when you are going to be out late; letting your hosts know where you are going so they can contact you in an emergency.

It is also usual to offer to help with household chores, for example, clearing the table and washing up the dishes after a meal, even if you are only visiting informally; and men are expected to offer, too. Your offer may or may not be accepted but at a more formal meal you will almost certainly be turned down.

If you're staying as the guest of a British family or even visiting for one meal, it is customary to take a small gift of flowers, chocolates or something to drink. Don't spend too much as this could embarrass your hosts. If you're staying for several days as a guest, it is usual to give a small present when you leave.

Usually you will get on first name terms with people you meet quite naturally and quickly. If you're unsure, continue to use their family name (surname) and title until they ask you to use their first name. Older people and those with whom you have a more formal relationship may prefer to stick to surnames (for example Dr Smith or Mrs Smith).

Meals

Most families have three meals a day but, if members of the family are working or studying, lunch is more likely to be eaten outside the home during the week. **Breakfast**, from 07.30 to 08.30, may be anything from bread, butter and marmalade (orange jam) to a cooked meal of bacon, eggs, sausage, tomato and mushrooms, fruit juice or cereal, followed by toast accompanied by tea or coffee. **Lunch**, between 12.00 and 14.00, is usually a light meal of soup, sandwiches or salad, cheese and fruit, although this may be different at the weekend. **Sunday lunch** is often the most important meal of the week, when a cooked meal, often including a joint of meat, is served at midday, instead of in the evening, and the whole family attends. On other days the main cooked meal is usually in the evening; either **high tea** when people return from work (around 18.30) or **dinner**, usually eaten later at about 19.30. In homes where a later dinner is usual this is often an adult meal; the children will probably eat much earlier when they return from school. Families who eat high tea in the evening may refer to lunch as their dinner so it might be best to check, if you're unsure, whether you've been invited to a midday or an evening meal. An evening meal may have a 'starter' course of soup or something light; the main course of meat or fish and vegetables followed by either a pudding, fruit and cheese, or, in the case of high tea, bread, cakes and tea. Supper is a lighter version of dinner. Supper and dinner are usually accompanied by soft drinks, beer or wine. You may also be offered alcoholic or non-alcoholic drinks before and after main meals, particularly in the evening.

If you do not eat meat or have special dietary needs let your hosts know in advance; there are plenty of vegetarians in Britain so it is not a difficult or unusual request.

The traditional British afternoon tea at home is a dying custom as there is often no one there at that time of day. But if people are home at about 16.00, for example at the weekend, you may be offered a cup of tea and sometimes bread and cakes as well. If you are invited to 'tea' usually some form of food is served.

Family life

If you would like to spend a few days with a British family, HOST, the British Association of the Experiment in International Living, the Universities and Colleges Christian Fellowship (UCCF) and the Victoria League for Commonwealth Friendship are organizations which can help you (their addresses are in Appendix 2).

EATING OUT

The British have acquired a taste for food from many different cultures and the first question is often, what kind of food do you feel like: Indian? Chinese? Italian? Vegetarian? One reason for the popularity of these types of restaurant is that they are often much cheaper than the more traditional British ones which serve a mixture of British and French cooking.

In the larger cities you will find almost every nationality represented by way of restaurants serving specialist or 'national' food. You would probably be wise, initially, to get someone to recommend a few places to suit your palate and your pocket (i.e. within your price range). People are often only too pleased to share new restaurant 'finds' with friends and acquaintances.

Take-away food

Restaurants often have a **take-away** service so you can buy cooked foods and take it to eat elsewhere. The most common are the American 'fast-food' hamburger restaurants, along with Indian, Chinese and Italian pizza take-aways. There are also increasing numbers of pizza delivery services so you don't even have to go out to the restaurant — you just phone through your order and pay when the pizza is brought to your door. The original British take-away food is fried fish and chips (potatoes/french fries) and there are still hundreds of fish and chip shops nation-wide. However, although you will find many of the other fast-food outlets open on a Sunday, it is illegal to sell fish and chips on a Sunday, so your local 'chippy' will most definitely be closed.

Self-service

Another cheap way to eat out is to go to a self-service café where you can serve yourself from a counter and pay for your food before eating it. Many self-service restaurants now offer a good range of salads and hot meals but some offer mainly fried food of the sausage, egg and chip variety. Motorway service stations usually offer a self-service restaurant amongst their facilities and, although they once had a poor reputation for the sort of food they offered and prices they charged for it, consumer pressure groups have forced a change. Nowadays you will find a reasonable variety of hot and cold foods available.

Restaurants

Restaurants with waiter service are usually more expensive than the places mentioned but beyond that it is impossible to generalize. Most restaurants display a menu outside the premises so you can see the type of food served and the range of prices. In restaurants there may be a cover charge, so much per head, and you will be expected to pay a 'service charge' or tip of at least ten per cent. Bear in mind, too, that drinks will usually cost more in a restaurant than in a shop or pub but most restaurants are licensed to serve alcohol whereas cheaper places are often not. Two things to check: usually menu prices include VAT, but make sure. Also check when the bill comes that a service charge has not already been added to it, otherwise you could end up paying it twice.

Drinking

Anyone may drink alcohol in Britain but you must be over eighteen to buy it or drink it on licensed premises. Places that sell alcohol have to be licensed and are governed by the licensing laws as to when they can open. English **public houses** or **'pubs'** are allowed to open between 11.00 and 23.00 except on Sundays when the hours are 12.00 to 15.00 and 19.00 to 22.30. However, individual landlords may choose their own hours within these limits and while pubs may be open during all available hours in cities, in rural areas more restricted times may be chosen. Scotland, Wales and Northern Ireland have their own but similar licensing laws and the opening and closing times vary slightly as a result. Some counties in Wales and some of the Scottish islands are 'dry' on Sunday, i.e., it is illegal to buy or sell alcohol on Sundays.

Pubs are an important part of British social life, where people meet and talk. **Beer** is traditionally the national drink. You may find it much heavier than beer at home — if you want a lighter beer, ask for lager. Pubs often serve food, particularly at lunchtime, which is usually cheap and tasty. A 'free house' is a pub which sells the beer of several different breweries; many pubs are owned by breweries and sell, mainly, their beer. In restaurants with a table licence, that is a licence to sell alcohol only with food, the licensing hours are longer and children of all ages can be admitted. Clubs also generally have special extended licences. Bars inside restaurants, hotels or other buildings, however, are governed by the same rules as pubs. **Off-licences** are special shops licensed to sell alcohol to be drunk off the premises. Many stick to pub hours but they can vary. Most supermarkets also have an off-licence section.

Drinking alcohol is not frowned upon in Britain, though getting very drunk is. Drunkenness, particularly if linked with driving, can get you arrested. Most people enjoy a drink either for its own sake or for social reasons and people will often meet in a pub or bar for a drink at lunchtime or perhaps in the early evening in between work and going home. People will also usually offer you a drink when you visit them at home or go to a party. In all these cases it is possible to ask for a non-alcoholic drink — never feel you have to have an alcoholic drink if you don't want to. If you feel strongly about going to places selling alcohol, make this clear to your British friends. There are usually alternative places where you can meet such as cafés. One alternative to the pub is the wine bar, where people generally drink wine or fruit juice rather than beer or spirits, and it has less of the atmosphere of heavy drinking than many pubs.

PUBLIC HOLIDAYS

There are eight public holidays in most of Britain (often referred to as **bank holidays** as these are the only weekdays when the banks close) plus some others which apply to Northern Ireland or Scotland only. The eight public holidays in England and Wales are:

New Year's Day	1 January
Good Friday Easter Monday	the days before and after the Easter weekend (in March/April)
Early May Bank Holiday	first Monday in May
Spring Bank Holiday	last Monday in May
Summer Bank Holiday	last Monday in August
Christmas Day	25 December
Boxing Day	26 December

SUMMARY — SOCIAL CUSTOMS

- *Visiting a British home* — the golden rule is to 'act thoughtfully'; offer to help with household chores like the washing up; take a small inexpensive gift for your host; use first names when you feel comfortable or are invited to do so.
- *Meals* — British people tend to have three meals a day — breakfast, lunch and the evening meal; the evening meal is usually the most important except

on Sundays when lunch may be the main 'activity'; if you have special dietary needs, let your hosts know in advance.

- *Eating out* — there is a huge variety of places to eat out in Britain; restaurants with waiter service tend to be more expensive than those offering take-away or self-service; get someone to recommend a few good and reasonably cheap places to eat out.
- *Drinking* — consumption of alcohol in Britain is strictly regulated e.g., places selling alcohol have to be licensed and you must be over eighteen to buy or drink it on licensed premises; the licensing laws also determine when pubs, wine bars, etc. may open; drunkenness is most definitely frowned upon and drinking and driving is illegal; never feel you have to have an alcoholic drink if you don't want one, there are plenty of alternatives readily available.
- *Public holidays* — there are eight public or 'bank' holidays in most of Britain plus some others which apply in Northern Ireland and Scotland only.

8
Sport and leisure opportunities

Britain has much to offer in addition to educational opportunities and in this chapter we indicate what is available in the way of sport and leisure. Participation in some of the activities described may help to broaden your experience and enjoyment of Britain, and help you to meet and make friends with British people.

THE ARTS

Cinemas and live theatre exist all over Britain. Although television has reduced their audiences, there are still over 1,500 cinemas. Most cities have at least one theatre, concert hall, museum and art gallery, although the theatre companies and orchestras which perform in them rely quite heavily on government subsidies from the Arts Council. Fringe theatre is a more recent development based on low-cost, short-term production. England, Scotland and Wales each have their own National Opera Company; there are permanent dance companies and symphony orchestras besides many smaller companies and, of course, Covent Garden for opera and ballet.

London has over a hundred commercial and subsidized theatres, including the highly-regarded National Theatre, in its own building in the South Bank arts complex, and the Royal Shakespeare Company in the Barbican arts complex. The RSC also has theatres in Stratford-upon-Avon (Shakespeare's birthplace).

London is particularly well served for concert halls, museums, art galleries and exhibitions, but several other towns hold annual arts or music festivals where, for a period of weeks, the range and standard of events is very impressive. Perhaps the best known of these is the Edinburgh Festival held annually each summer. Some of the major theatre, opera and ballet companies and orchestras also do regional tours and almost every town also has its amateur theatrical, operatic and music societies. There are often reduced-price tickets for students.

SPORTS AND GAMES

There are very few sports which it is not possible to practise in Britain. All forms of water sports, sailing and rowing are practised on our lakes, rivers and coastline, although the climate tends to make these more popular in summer. Walking, rock climbing, mountaineering and horse riding are all good ways to explore the landscape. Nearer to home you will almost certainly find outdoor pitches for football, cricket and other team games and athletics grounds. Tennis is played on outdoor courts in the summer while squash has become a popular game in recent years as it can be played year-round on indoor courts. Most colleges and towns also have indoor swimming pools and some have ice-skating rinks. Many colleges have their own extremely impressive sports facilities and this is the best place to start finding out what is available, especially during freshers' week.

Less active indoor sports include snooker (a popular spectator sport on television at the moment) or more sedentary games such as bridge or chess (there is often a local bridge club and chess club). The most popular spectator sports are football and horse racing. Most large towns have their own football team and ground while race courses are found in the country and outside most major cities. All forms of motor racing are also popular.

If your college does not offer much in the way of sports facilities, try the local town hall or public library as many of the facilities mentioned are provided by the public authority and for most popular sports it is not necessary to have to join expensive private clubs. Some towns have sport centres where a number of indoor and outdoor facilities are provided in a pleasant social atmosphere.

EVENING CLASSES

If you wish to take up a new hobby, a sport or interest or even improve an existing one, there is a huge range of evening classes offered by your local Adult Education authority. Details of courses are available from local education authorities, colleges or the British Council. Courses are charged by the hour though you generally have to enrol for a seven- or eight-week term. The sorts of courses you are likely to find on offer include art, drama, music, crafts, languages, domestic skills and social, academic and professional subjects ranging from accountancy and acrobatics to woodwork, world affairs and yoga. Fifty eight different kinds of dancing class are available, from African folk dance and ballet to disco dancing and modern jazz. There is a national popular interest in doing exercise classes to music (aerobics) and you may prefer this kind of exercise to sport. Evening classes are a good way, especially for spouses, to meet people.

TOURING BRITAIN

Despite its small size, Britain has a varied landscape, ranging from the flat countryside in Norfolk to the Welsh mountains, the Scottish Highlands and the mountainous English Lake District. Besides its coastline and fine beaches, there are many natural rivers and man-made waterways which are navigable by boat. In the less mountainous parts there is gentler scenery, rolling hills and downs with rich farmlands where much of the fresh fruit, vegetables and other food crops we need are grown, and there is beautiful countryside within easy reach of even the major industrial towns.

Many towns date back to before Roman times and there are fascinating archaeological sites all over the country. The smallest village may have a fine early church; cathedrals, abbeys and churches have often survived in places where other buildings have been replaced many times over. Older towns often retain their original fortified walls and castles, many now in ruins. Britain is also famous for its 'country houses', the beautiful country homes landowners built for themselves when civil strife became less common and castles unnecessary. The British have always been keen gardeners and in many cases the grounds and gardens of some houses are worth a visit in their own right.

Staying away from home need not be expensive. Many farmhouses and homes at seaside and holiday towns offer 'bed and breakfast' (a sort of tourist equivalent to student lodgings) and there are many cheap 'guest houses' and hotels, particularly if you can travel outside the main holiday seasons. If you would like to stay with a family, the National Tourist Information Centre at Victoria station and the British Tourist Authority (BTA) 'Meet the British' leaflet lists some agencies and individual families who can arrange for you to stay in their homes for as little as £17 a night, anywhere from Cornish cottages to Scottish castles. Alternatively, try the hundreds of registered camping or caravan sites (you can hire caravans and equipment) or hire a boat and go by water. If you want to camp on private land you must get the owner's consent first, though, and if you plan to go at a busy time of year you may need to book ahead. Finally, always check your insurance covers what you plan to do or whether you need to take out special holiday insurance.

For hotel, guest-house, restaurant, sight-seeing and tourist guides and maps contact a Tourist Information Centre (see also page 74) where you are living in Britain. You could also visit the National Tourist Information Centre at Victoria station and the Youth Hostel Association. England, Scotland, Wales and Northern Ireland each have their own official tourist board (addresses in Appendix 2).

London Briefing (from the London Conference, address in Appendix 2) gives details of how to find out about leisure activities in the London area. Some COSAs and International Societies in other towns also produce booklets or information packs (their addresses are in Appendix 2). These are only available to students after their arrival in Britain.

HOLIDAYS ABROAD

Students from other continents will find Britain makes a good base from which to explore Europe or further afield. You can either make your own travel arrangements, taking advantage of student fares, and rely on finding the sort of accommodation you can afford when you arrive, or you may find it less risky and quite economical to book a 'package tour', where your travel and accommodation are booked in advance for you as a package, usually at a cheaper all-in-price than if you had paid for them separately. The students' union at your college can advise on student travel insurance (always wise if you are going abroad). Otherwise, holiday firms advertise very heavily in national daily and weekly papers or you can ask your local travel agent to make the arrangements; it is wise to go to a travel agent who is a member of the Association of British Travel Agents (ABTA). If you want to take your car abroad, seek advice from one of the motoring organizations like the AA or RAC (addresses in Appendix 2).

Re-entry documents

As well as checking what documents you need for the countries you propose to visit, you may need a re-entry visa to return to Britain. If you needed a visa to enter Britain initially, you will need similar documents to show Immigration on your return. This requires a good deal of advance planning.

First, check in your passport that your permission to stay in Britain is not due to expire for at least two months (longer if you plan to stay away longer). Renewal of permission can take at least two months so you won't be able to apply for a re-entry visa unless your permission to stay is extended first. If you have two months or less left on your passport, renew it immediately (see page 44). Once you have permission to stay in Britain long enough to cover your holiday and your return, you can apply for a re-entry visa from the Passport Office, Clive House, Petty France, London SW1H 9HD, or any other British passport office, but you need to do this at least a month before you intend to leave Britain.

On your return, as well as your re-entry visa, you will need:

- a letter from your college confirming you are still registered as a full-time student there and will be returning at the end of your holiday to resume the course;
- evidence of sufficient funds to support you in Britain for a further period.

If it is impossible to get a re-entry visa before your departure you may apply while you are on holiday abroad, from the nearest official British representative. But if you plan to do this, remember to take away with you the necessary proof of full-time study and funds.

Most Commonwealth students (see page 22) and holders of Home Office letters of consent whose studies are continuing do not need re-entry visas, but do need to carry the letter from their college and to have evidence of sufficient funds.

SUMMARY — SPORT AND LEISURE OPPORTUNITIES

- *The arts* — the arts are well represented all over Britain so you don't have to be based in London to take advantage of what is on offer; you will often find reduced-price tickets for students.
- *Sports and games* — there are lots of sports you can take part in in Britain; your college during freshers' week is the best place to start finding out what is on offer in your local area, otherwise the local library or town hall should have the information you need.
- *Evening classes* — to find out what is available and how much it will cost get in touch with the local Adult Education authority; evening classes are an excellent way, especially for spouses, of getting to meet people.
- *Touring Britain* — if you want to use your college vacations to travel around

and see more of Britain it need not be expensive; the National Tourist Information Centre at Victoria station, London, and the British Tourist Authority are good starting points.

- *Holidays abroad* — again these may be cheaper than you think; you can either make your own arrangements or go through an ABTA travel agent; remember to take out travel insurance and, if you are taking a car, get advice from one of the motoring organizations; check whether you are going to need a re-entry visa and if so allow yourself plenty of time to make the necessary arrangements; make sure you also have evidence of funding and a letter from your college confirming that you are still registered as a full-time student and will return to resume your studies at the end of your holiday — you will need both to clear Immigration on your return.

CONCLUSION

We hope that this book has achieved its aim of providing you with enough basic information on the educational, financial and social aspects of studying and living in Britain to help you decide first, whether you want to come to study here, and second, how best to plan to make your stay as comfortable and enjoyable as possible. If, however, there are any ways you feel the book can be improved, please let the British Council know and we will try to incorporate your ideas in future editions.

Finally, when you have completed your studies and are thinking about making arrangements to return home, bear in mind that most countries require foreign educational certificates acquired in another country to be authenticated — that is, certified to be genuine. To save yourself trouble and delay later, arrange authentication of your British qualifications certificates before you leave. Your consular representative in Britain should be able to advise you on your country's particular requirements.

We wish you every success with your studies.

Britain showing universities, polytechnics and Scottish Central Institutions

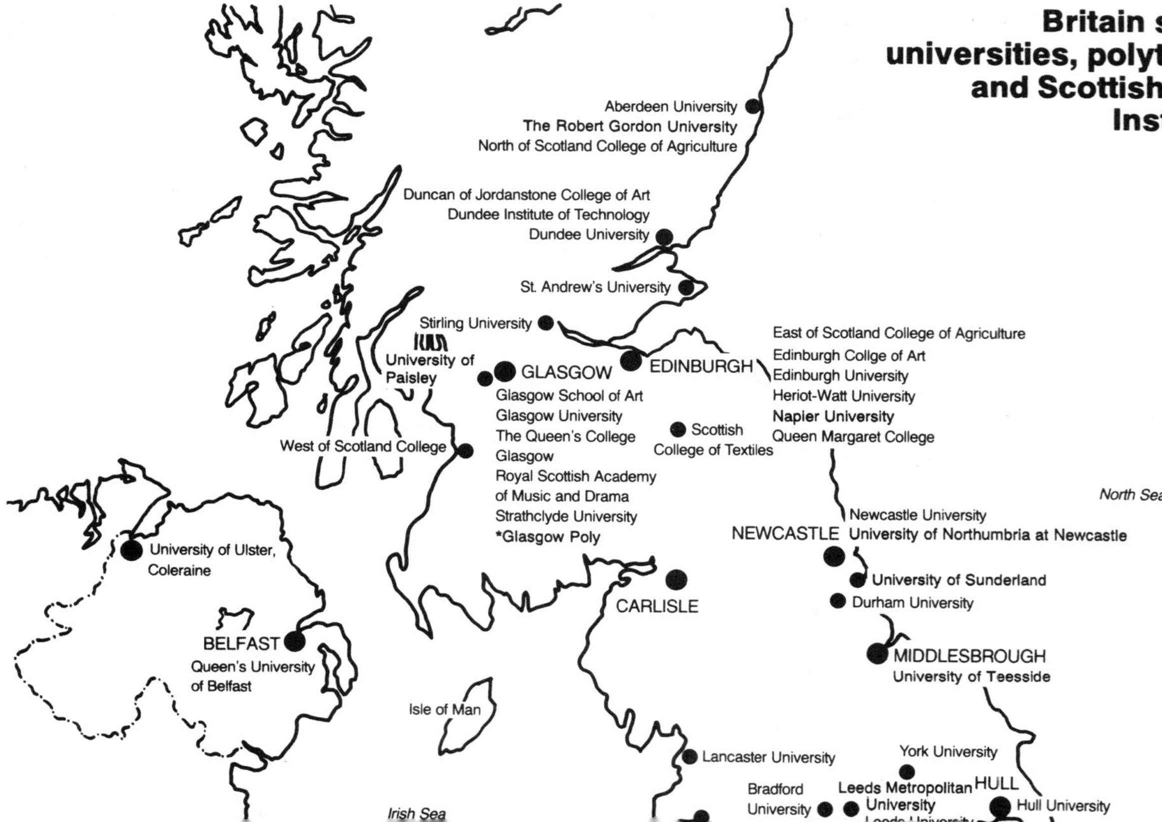

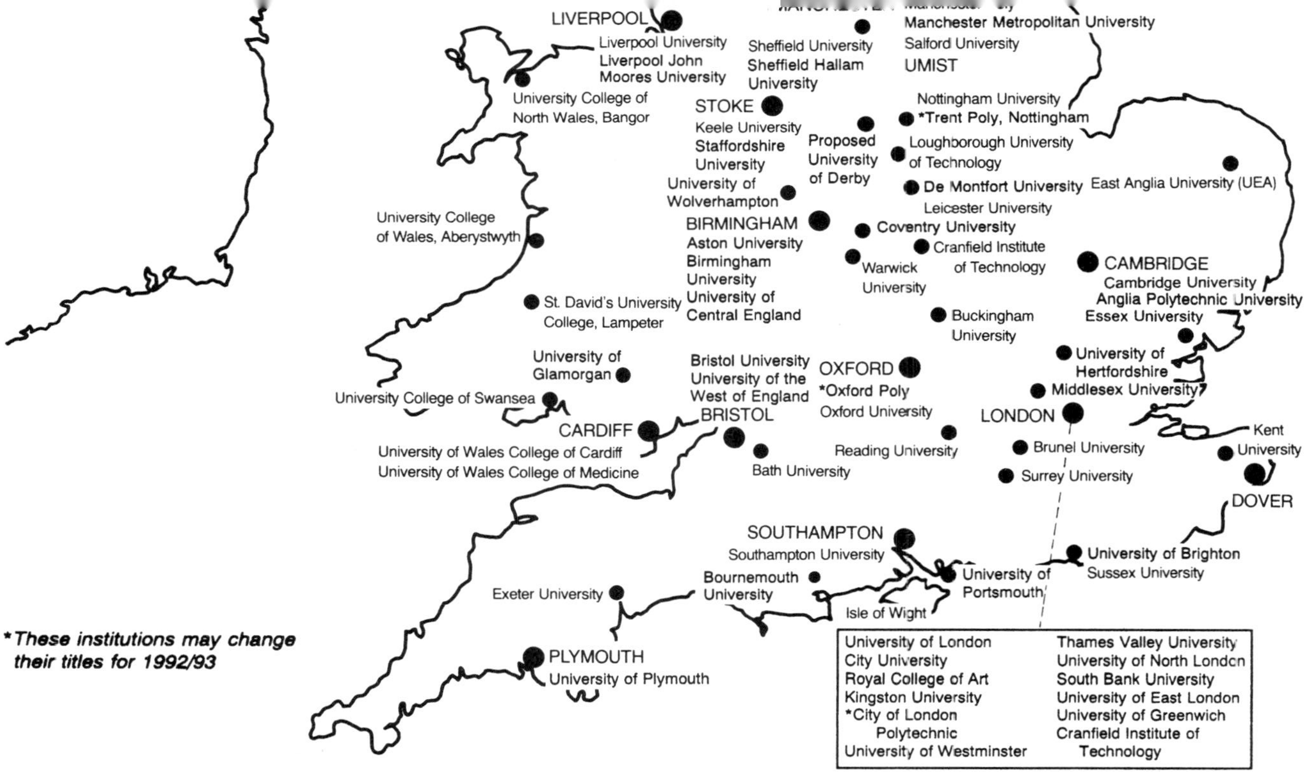

**These institutions may change their titles for 1992/93*

There are over 800 institutes of further and higher education whose location cannot be included on the map.

CHART E: SOURCES OF HELP

General (for advice on educational and travel arrangements particularly)	The British Council in your home country or in Britain (addresses listed in Appendix 1)
Meeting/temporary accommodation Temporary accommodation	The British Council Arrivals Group, 10 Spring Gardens, London SW1A 2BN The London Tourist Board & Convention Bureau Tourist Information Centre (addresses in Appendix 2)
Immigration	UK Immigrants Advisory Service (UKIAS) Joint Council for the Welfare of Immigrants (JCWI) (addresses listed in Appendix 2) your college welfare officer
Accommodation	your college accommodation officer or, in London, The British Council Accommodation Unit (address in Appendix 1)
General — relating to any legal problems over e.g. housing/landlords, consumer goods and information, particularly on state services General — particularly student welfare, insurance, travel and other discounts, academic matters	Citizens Advice Bureau (local addresses in your telephone directory) National Union of Students (NUS) officer at your college
Health — registration with a doctor or with a student health service	British Council Programme Officer if you are on an award administered by the British Council Local Family Practitioner Committee (England and Wales), local health board or local health council (Scotland), or Central Services Agency (Northern Ireland) (addresses in local telephone directory) a list of local doctors (GPs) at the main post office or public library in your area
Motoring	Automobile Association and Royal Automobile Club (address in local telephone directory and Appendix 2)
Social/tourism	Local Conference on Overseas Students (COSAs) (addresses available from UKCOSA; see Appendix 2) British Tourist Authority (see Appendix 2) and the national tourist boards (addresses available from Tourist Information Centre; see Appendix 2)
Emergency — fire brigade, police, ambulance	dial 999 and ask for the service you need (free from public and private telephones)

Appendix 1

BRITISH COUNCIL OFFICES IN BRITAIN AND OVERSEAS, 1993

British Council Offices in Britain 1993

Bangor
Programme Officer
3rd Floor
Students Union Building
University College of North Wales
Deiniol Road
Bangor LL57 2TH
Tel: (0248) 364025/351107
Ext. 2882

Belfast
Director
1 Chlorine Gardens
Belfast BT9 5DJ
Tel: (0232) 666770/706

Birmingham
Director
2nd Floor
Burnley House
13 Temple Street
(Second Floor)
Birmingham B2 5BN
Tel: (021) 632 5482

Brighton
Director
London Gate
72 Dyke Road Drive
Brighton BN1 6AJ
Tel: (0273) 542411

Bristol
Director
7 Priory Road
Tyndall's Park
Bristol BS8 1UA
Tel: (0272) 738466

Cambridge
Director
Bishop Bateman Court
5-7 New Park Street
Cambridge CB5 8AT
Tel: (0223) 354786

Cardiff
Director
28 Park Place
Cardiff CF1 3QE
Tel: (0222) 397346

Edinburgh
Director
3 Bruntsfield Crescent
Edinburgh EH10 4HD
Tel: (031) 447 4716

Glasgow
Director
6 Belmont Crescent
Glasgow G12 8ES
Tel: (041) 339 8651

Leeds
Director
1 St Mark's Avenue
Leeds LS2 9BJ
Tel: (0532) 445211

London
Headquarters South
British Council
10 Spring Gardens
London SW1A 2BN
Tel: 071-930 8466
including London Regional Office, Accommodation Unit and the London Conference on Overseas Students

Manchester

Headquarters North
The British Council
Medlock Street
Manchester M15 4PR
Tel: (061) 957 7000

Newcastle upon Tyne
Director
13 Windsor Terrace
Jesmond
Newcastle upon Tyne
NE2 4HE
Tel: (091) 281 4366

Nottingham
Director
8 Sherwood Rise
Nottingham NG7 6JF
Tel: (0602) 621939

Oxford
Director
1 Beaumont Place
Oxford OX1 2PJ
Tel: (0865) 57236

Reading
Programme Officer
The University
Whiteknights Road
P O Box 238
Reading RG6 2AL
Tel: (0734) 751807/313014/
875123. Ext 4103.

Southampton
Programme Officer
61 University Road
Highfield
Southampton SO9 5NH
Tel: (0703) 558516

For students whose awards are administered by the British Council, there are outposted student support offices in Aberdeen, Dundee, Hull, Leicester, Liverpool, Loughborough, Sheffield and Swansea.

British Council offices overseas, 1993

Algeria
Director
6 Avenue Souidani Boudjemaa
Algiers
Tel: 60 55 22, 60 56 82
Telex: 66197 BRICO DZ
Fax: 590981

Argentina
Director
Martcelot de Alvear 590-4
1508 Buenos Aires
Tel: 3119814
Telex: 18728 BRICON
Fax: 3117747

Australia
Director
Edgecliff Centre
203/233 New South Head Road
(PO Box 88)
Edgecliff, Sydney
NSW 2027
Tel: 326 2022
Telex: 24769 BCSYD AA
Fax: 3274868

Austria
Director
Schenkenstrasse 4
A-1010 Vienna
Tel: 533 26 16/7/8
Telex: 132521 BC VIE A
Fax: 533 26 1685

Bahrain
Director
Shaikh Salman Highway
(PO Box 452)
Manama 306
Tel: 261555
Telex: 9509 BRICON
Fax: 241272

Bangladesh
Director
5 Fuller Road
(PO Box 161)
Dhaka 1000
Tel: 500107/8/9
Telex: 642470 BRICO BJ
Fax: 863375

Librarian
Laldighi South
Chittagong
Tel: 223632

Librarian
Malopara
(PO Box 9)
Rajshahi
Tel: 2185

Barbados (see Caribbean)

Belgium and Luxembourg
Director
Britannia House
Rue Joseph II/Jozef II Straat,30
1040 Brussels
Tel: 2 19 36 00
Telex: 24743 BCBELB
Fax: 2175811

Botswana
Director
British High Commission
Building
Queen's Road
The Mall
(PO Box 439)
Gaborone
Tel: 353602
Telex 2368 BRICO BD
Fax: 356643

Brazil
Director
SCR 708/9-BLF
Nos 1/3
(Caixa Postal 6104)
70.740 Brasilia DF
Tel: 272 3060
Telex: 611859 BCOU BR
Fax: 272 3455

Director North-East
Avenue Domingos Ferreira 4150
Boa Viagem
(Caixa Postal 4079)
51021 Recife PE
Tel: 326 6640
Telex: 814014 BCOU BR
Fax: 326 4880

Director Rio de Janeiro
Rua Elmano Cardim 10
Urca
(Caixa Postal 2237)
22291 Rio de Janeiro RJ
Tel: 295 7782
Telex: 2130244 BCOU BR
Fax: 541 3693

Director São Paulo
Rua Maranhao 416
Higienópolis
(Caixa Postal 1604)
01240 São Paulo SP
Tel: 826 4455
Telex: 1126 286 COBT BR
Fax: 66 3765

Brunei
Director
Hong Kong Bank Chambers
Jalan Pemancha
(PO Box 3049)
Bandar Seri Begawan 1930
Negara Brunei Darussalam
Tel: 227531/480
Telex: 2211 UKREP BU
Fax: 241769

Bulgaria
Director
7 Tulovo Street
Sofia 1504
Tel: 244 3394
Telex: 24212 BRITCO BG
Fax: 462065

Burkina Faso
see Côte d'Ivoire

Burma
Cultural Attaché
British Embassy
80 Strand Road
(PO Box 638)
Rangoon
Tel: 81700-2/81708/81812/81138
Telex: 21216 PRODRM BM
(Embassy)
Fax: 95189566 (Embassy)

Cameroon
Director
Immeuble Christo
rue Charles de Gaulle
(BP 818)
Yaoundé
Tel: 203172
Fax: 215691
Telex: 8408 BRICONKN

Canada
Director
c/o British High Commission
80 Elgin Street
Ottawa
Ontario K1P 5K7
Tel: 237 1530
Telex: 533318 UK REP OTT
Fax: 237 7980 (High
Commission)

Director Montreal
British Consulate-General
1155 University Street
Montreal
Quebec H3B 3A7
Tel: 866 5863
Telex: 556 1244 BRITAIN MTL
Fax: 866 0202

Cape Verde
See Senegal

Caribbean
Director
First Life Building
64 Knutsford Boulevard
(PO Box 575)
Kingston 5
Jamaica
Tel: 92-96915
Telex: 3698 BCON
Fax: (809) 92 970 90

Liaison Officer
British High Commission
Furness House
90 Independence Square
(PO Box 778)
Port of Spain
Trinidad
Tel: 62 528616
Telex: 22224
Fax: 623 0621

Chile
Director
Eliodoro Yanex 832
Casilla 15-T Tajamar
Santiago
Tel: 2234622/2234739
Telex: 341183 CONBRCK
Fax: 460005

China
Counsellor (Cultural)
4th Floor
Landmark Building
8 North Dongsanhaun Road
Chaoyang District
Beijing 100026

First Secretary (Cultural)
South China
Room 1202
Easey Commercial Building
255 Hennessy Road
Hong Kong
Tel: 8315135/6
Telex 74141 BCOUN HX
Fax: 8385563

Consul (Cultural)
British Consulate-General
Qi Hua Tower 5B
1375 HuaiHai Zhong Lu
Shanghai 200031
Tel: 4714849
Telex: 33476 BRIT CN
Fax: 433 3115

Colombia
Director
Calle 87 Nos 12/79
(Apartado Aéreo 089231)
Bogotá DE
Tel: 236 3882, 236 3976
Telex 45715 BCOUN CO
Fax: 2187754

Croatia
Director
Ilica 12/1
(PO Box 55)
41000 Zagreb
Tel: 041 273491/2
Telex: 22533 BRIZAG RH
Fax: 041 421725

Cyprus
Director
3 Museum Street
(PO Box 5654)
Nicosia
Tel: 442152, 442371
Telex: 3911 BRICONIC CY
Fax: 477257

Czechoslovakia
Narodni 10
113 19 Prague 1
Tel: 203751-5,224501
Telex: 29 44 48 (a/b BCCZ C)
Fax: 2058 63

Bratislavia (Slovakia)
Panska 17
811 01 Bratislava

Denmark
Director Nordic Area
Møntergade 1
1116 Copenhagen K
Tel: 33 11 20 44
Telex: REF BCO023, 265451
MONREF G
Fax: 33321501

East Jerusalem and Gaza
Director
(PO Box 19136)
31 Nablus Road
Jerusalem
Tel: 282545, 282863;
English Language Centre
271131, 894392
Telex: 26394 BCEJMIL
Fax: 283021

Office Manager
House 54-279
Orabi Street
Al Rimal
(PO Box 355)
Gaza
Tel: 86246
Telex and fax via E. Jerusalem

Ecuador
Director
Avenue Amazonas 1646
Orellana
(Casilla 8829)
Quito
Tel: 540 225/232 421/231 686
Telex: 22842 CONBRI ED
Fax: 565720

DTO Manager
Costanera 504
entre Las Monjas y Ebanos
(PO Box 6547)
Guayaquil

Egypt
Director
192 Sharia el Nil, Agouza
Cairo
Tel: 2453281-4, 3476188
Telex: 21534 BRICO UN
Fax. 3443076

Director Alexandria
9 Batalsa Street
Bab Shark
Alexandria
Tel: 482 0199/9890
Telex: 55657 BC ALX UN

Ethiopia
Director
Artistic Building
Adwa Avenue
(PO Box 1043)
Addis Ababa
Tel: 55 00 22/24/28/90
Telex: 21561 BC ET
Fax: 552544

Librarian
No. 23 Lorenzo Taazag Street
(PO Box 997)
Asmara
Tel: 113415

Fiji
see South Pacific

Finland
Director
Hakaniemenkatu 2
00530 Helsinki
Tel: 7018731
Fax: 701 8725

France
Director
9 Rue de Constantine
75007 Paris
Tel: 49 55 73 00
Telex: 250912 BRICOUN F
Fax: 47 05 77 02

Germany
Director
Hahnenstrasse 6
5000 Cologne 1
Tel: 20 64 40
Telex: 888 1147 BCGK D
Fax: 20 64 455

Director Eastern Germany
Hardenbergstrasse 20
1000 Berlin 12
Tel: 31 10 99
Telex: 185814 BCGB D
Fax: 31 10 99-20

Director Northern Germany
Rothenbaumchaussee 34
2000 Hamburg 13
Tel: 44 60 57/8
Telex: 2162557 BCHB D
Fax: 447114

Director Southern Germany
Rosenheimer Strasse 116b
Haus 93 (Kustermann-Park)
8000 Munich 80
Tel: 40 18 32
Fax: 40 56 69

Ghana
Director
Liberia Road
(PO Box 771)
Accra
Tel: 224773
Telex: 2369 BRICO GH

Office Manager
Bank Road
(PO Box 1996)
Kumasi
Tel: 051 3462
Telex: 2369 BRICO GH

Greece
Director
Plateia Philikis
Etairias 17
Kolanaki Square
Athens 10210
(PO Box 3488)
Tel: 36 33211/3606011
Telex: 218 799 BRIC GR
Fax: 3634769

Director Thessaloniki
Ethnikis Amynis 9
(PO Box 50007)
54013 Thessaloniki
Tel: 235236, 285570
Telex: 412974 BCSLGR
Fax: 282498

Guinea (Conakry) and Guinea-Bissau – See Senegal

Hong Kong
Director
Easey Commercial Building
255 Hennessy Road Wanchai
Hong Kong
Tel: 8795138
Telex: 74141 BCOUN HX
Fax: 8345731, 8346759 (ECS)
5729689 (Exchanges)

Hungary
Director
Budapest VI
Benczur Utca 26
H-1068
Tel: 121 5149
Telex: 224527 BRIT H
Fax: 142 5728

India
Minister (Cultural Affairs)
British High Commission
British Council Division
AIFACS Building
Rafi Marg
New Delhi 110/001
Tel: 3711401, 382004, 3710555
Telex: 3165460 BCND IN
Fax: 3782016

First Secretary (Cultural Affairs)
British Deputy High Commission
British Council Division
Mittal Tower 'C' Wing
Nariman Point
Bombay 400 021
Tel: 223530 2235560
Telex: 116991 BCBY IN
Fax: 2852024

First Secretary
(Cultural Affairs)
British Deputy High Commission
British Council Division
5 Shakespeare Sarani
Calcutta 700 071
Tel: 225370, 225378-9
Telex: 215984 BCCA IN
Fax: 224804

First Secretary
(Cultural Affairs)
British Deputy High Commission
British Council Division
737 Anna Salai
Madras 600 002
Tel: 89402/3/4/5
Telex: 417775 BCMS IN

Indonesia
Representative
S Widjojo Centre
Jalan Jenderal Sudirman 71
Jakarta 12190
Tel: 5223250
Telex: 45246 BRICON JKT
Fax: 5223106

Librarian
Jalan Lembong 4 A-6
Bandung
Tel: 50788

Librarian
Jalan Jen a Yani No 2
Medan
Tel: 519 992

Iraq
Director
Waziriya 301
Street 3
Houses 22 and 24
(PO Box 298)
Baghdad
Tel: 4220091/2
Telex: 212773 BRICON IK
Fax: 4255601

Ireland
Director
22/24 Lower Mount Street
Dublin 2
Tel: 764088/766943
Fax: 766945

Israel
Director
140 Hayarkon Street
Tel Aviv 61032
Tel: 222 194/242 558
Telex: 35537BCTAIL
Fax: 221 229

Librarian/Office Manager
3 Ethiopia Street
(PO Box 32174)
Jerusalem 91320
Tel: 250153, 250597
Fax: 250153

Italy
Director
Palazzo del Drago
Via Quattro Fontane 20
00184 Rome
Tel: 4826641/8
Telex: 622231 BRICON I
Fax: 481 4296

Director Bologna
Casa Isolani
Strada Maggiore 19
40125 Bologna

Director Milan
Via Manzoni 38
20121 Milan
Tel: 782018 782016, 781749
Telex: 311084 BRICON I
Fax: 781119

Director Naples
Palazzo d'Avalos
Via Dei Mille 48
80 121 Naples
Tel: 414876/421321
Telex: 710460 BRICON I
Fax: 42 69 62

Jamaica
See Caribbean

Japan
Director
2-Kagurazaka 1-chome
Shinjuku-ku
Tokyo 162
Tel: 03235 8031
Telex: J27761 BRITCOUN
Fax: 032358040

Director Kyoto
77 Kitashirakawa
Nishi-Machi
Sakyo-ku
Kyoto 606
Tel: 075791, 7151/2
Fax: 0757917154

Jordan
Director
Rainbow Street (off First Circle)
Jabal Amman
(PO Box 634)
Amman
Tel: 63147/8/638194, 624686
Telex: 21823 BCJORJO
Fax: 9626 656413

Kenya
Director
ICEA Building
Kenyatta Avenue
(PO Box 40751)
Nairobi
Tel: 334855/6/7/334928, 334983
Telex: 23212 BRITCOUN
Fax: 339 854

Korea
Director
Anglican Church Annex
3/7 Chung Dong
Choong-ku
Seoul
Tel: 737 7157/7265/738 7452
Telex: 29426 BRICON K
Fax: 737 9911

Kuwait
Director
2 al Arabi Street
(PO Box 345)
Mansouriyah
Tel: 2533204/2515512/2533227
Telex: 22022 KT
Fax: 2551376

Lesotho
Director
Hobson's Square
(PO Box 429)
Maseru 100
Tel: 312609/10
Telex: 4239 BRITCOLO
Fax: 310636

Madagascar
see Mauritius

Malawi
Director
Plot No 13/20
City Centre
(PO Box 30222)
Lilongwe 3
Tel: 730266/7/8
Telex: 4476 BRICOUN MI
Fax: 731062

Office Manager
Henderson Street
(PO Box 456)
Blantyre
Tel: 620207

Malaysia
Jalan Bukit Aman
(PO Box 10539)
50916 Kuala Lumpur
Tel: 2987 555/690/791/892
Telex 31052 BRICO MA
Fax: 2937214

Director East Malaysia
Bangunan Ang Cheng Go
Jalan Tunku Abdul Rahman
93100 Kuching
Sarawak
East Malaysia
Tel: 256271, 256044, 242632
Fax: 425199

Officer-in-Charge
Wing On Life Building
1 Lorong Sagunting
(PO Box 10746)
88808 Kota Kinabalu
Sabah
East Malaysia
Tel: 248055, 248298
Telex: 80337 BRITCO MA
Fax: 238059

Director Penang
43 Greenhall
(PO Box 595)
10770 Penang
Malaysia
Tel: 630330, 630332, 630391
Telex: 31052 BRICO MA
Fax: 633589

Maldive Islands
see Sri Lanka

Mali and Mauritania
see Senegal

Malta
English Language Adviser
89 Archbishop Street
Valetta
Tel: 224707
Fax: 243366

Mauritius
Director
Royal Road
(PO Box 111)
Rose Hill
Tel: 4549551
Fax: 4549553

Mexico
Director
Maestro Antonio Caso 127
Col San Rafael
(Apdo Postal 30-588)
Mexico City 06470 DF
Tel: 566-6144/6595/6743/6187/6384
Telex: 1772938 BRICO ME
Fax: 535 5984

Morocco
Director
36 rue de Tangier
(BP 427)
Rabat
Tel: 60836, 60850
Telex: 31022 PRODROME M
Fax: 60850

Mozambique
Director
Travessa da Catembe 21
(PO Box 4178)
Maputo
Tel: 421571/3/4
Telex: 6845 BRICO MO
Fax: 421577

Namibia
Director
74 Bulowstrasse
(PO Box 24224)
Windhoek 9000
Telephone: 226776
Telex: 090 8892 BRCOU WK
Fax: 227530

Nepal
Director
Kantipath
(PO Box 640)
Kathmandu
Tel: 221305,223796, 223000
Telex: 2382 BRICON NP
Fax: 224076

Netherlands
Director
Keizersgracht 343
1016 EH Amsterdam
Tel: 622 36 44
Telex: 16599 BCAMS NL
Fax: 207389

New Zealand
Director
c/o British High Commission
44 Hill Street
(PO Box 1812)
Wellington 1
Tel: 4726049
Telex: 3325 UKREP NZ (High Commission)
Fax: 4736261

Niger
see Côte d'Ivoire

Nigeria
Director
11 Kingsway Road
Ikoyi
(PO Box 3702)
Lagos
Tel: 610210/603690/5
Telex: 22071 BRICO NG
Fax: 618202

Director Enugu
Teachers' House
Ogui Road
(PO Box 330)
Enugu
Tel: 330158, 338456, 335577, 335677
Telex: via Lagos

Director Kaduna
Hospital Road
(PO Box 81)
Kaduna
Tel: 201080/1
Telex: 71159 BRITCO NG

Director Kano
10 Kofar Nassarawa
(PMB 3003 Kano)
Kano City
Tel: 626652/2500
Telex: via Kaduna

Norway
Director
Fridtjof Nansens Plass 5
0160 Oslo 1
Tel: 42 68 48
Telex: 79421 BRICON
Fax: 424039

Oman
Director
Medinat Qaboos West
(PO Box 7090 Muttrah)
Tel: 600548
Telex: 5718 BRITCOUN ON
Fax: 699163

Director, English Language Centre
(PO Box 18249)
Salalah
Tel: 292080
Fax: 294854

Pakistan
Director
23, 87th Street G 6/3
(PO Box 1135)
Islamabad
Tel: 822502/5, 822670,820153/4
Telex: 5641 BRICO PK
Fax: 822670

Director Karachi
20 Bleak House Road
(PO Box 10410)
Karachi 0406
Tel: 512036/8, 513694
Telex: 25570 BRICO PK

Director Lahore
65 Mozang Road
(PO Box 88)
Lahore
Tel: 52755/6, 54278
Telex: 44337 BRICO PK
Fax: 368674

Area Officer
35 Sharah-e-Quaid-e-Azam
(PO Box 49)
Peshawar
Tel: 73278, 75056

Peru
Director
Calle Alberto Lynch 110
San Isidro
(Apartado 14-0114
Sucursal Sta Beatriz)
Lima 14
Tel: 704350
Telex: 21510 BRITCOUN PE
Fax: 704380

Philippines
Director
7, 3rd Street
New Manila
(PO Box AC 168, Cubao)
Quezon City
Metro Manila
Tel: 7211981/4
Telex: 67789 BRITCOUN PN
Fax: 7211336

Poland
Director
Al Jerozolimskie 59
00-697 Warsaw
Tel: 6287401/3
Telex: 812555 BRIN PL

Portugal
Director
Rua de São Marçal 174
(1294 Lisbon Codex)
Tel: 347 6141/7
Telex: 42544 BRITCO P
Fax: 347 6152

Director Coimbra
Casa de Inglatera
Rua de Tomar 4
3000 Coimbra
Tel: 39 23549
Telex: 52435 BRICOIP

Director Oporto
Rua de Breyner 155
4000 Oporto
Tel: 2005577
Telex: 29297 BRIOPOP
Fax: 2084762

Qatar
Director
Ras Abu Aboud Road
(PO Box 2292)
Doha
Tel: 4262193/4/426185
Telex: 4608 BRITCO DH
Fax: 320065

Romania
Cultural Attaché
Calea Dorob-Antilor 14
Bucharest
Tel: 120310
Telex: 11295 PRODM R (Embassy)
Fax:120310

Russian Federation
Cultural Section
British Embassy Moscow
Ulyanovskaya Ulitsa
Dum 1, (VGBIL)
Moscow 109189
Tel: 2973499
Telex: 413441 BEMOS SU (Embassy)
Fax: 095 2333563 (Cultural Section)

Saudi Arabia
Director
Olaya Main Road
Al Mousa Centre
Tower B
(PO Box 58012)
Riyadh 11594
Tel: 462 1818, 464 4928
Telex: 400565 BRICON SJ
Fax: 462 0063

Director Jeddah
Middle East Centre, 4th Floor
Falasteen Street
(PO Box 3424)
Jeddah 21471
Tel: 672 3336, 672 6341
Telex: 603962 BRCOUN SJ
Fax: 672 6341

Senegal
Director
34/36 Blvd de la République
Immeuble Sonotel
(BP 6232)
Dakar
Tel: 22 20 15, 22 20 48
Telex: 21709 BRICO SG
Fax: 221 218136

Seychelles
see Mauritius

Sierra Leone
Director
Tower Hill
(PO Box 124)
Freetown
Tel: 222223, 222227, 224683, 224684
Telex: 3453 BRICON SL
Fax: 24123

Singapore
Director
30 Napier Road
Singapore 1025
Tel: 473 1111
Telex: 20456 BRICO RS
Fax: 4721010

South Africa
Director
76 Juta Street
(PO Box 30637)
Braamfontein 2017
Johannesburg
Tel: 339 3715
Telex: 426428 BRISA
Fax: 339 7806

Director Cape Town
Suite 501
Main Tower
Cape Town Centre
Foreshore
Cape Town 8001
Tel: 4196050
Telex: 523288
Fax: 211502

South Pacific
Education and Training Adviser
British Development Division in the South Pacific
Vanua House
Victoria Parade
Suva
Fiji
Tel: 312286
Telex: 2289 BDDP SUVA FJ
Fax: 301218

Spain
Director
Calle Almagro 5
28010 Madrid
Tel: 337 3500
Telex: 42769 INSBR E
Fax: 337 3573

Director Barcelona
Calle Amigo 83
08021 Barcelona
Tel: 209 13 64/ 63 88/ 60 90
Telex: 50512 BINB E
Fax: 202 31 68

Director Bilbao
British Institute
Residentia Universitaria
Estaban Terradas
Plaza de la Casilla 3
48012 Bilbao
Tel: 444 66 66
Fax: 444 60 30

Director Oviedo
British Institute
Calle del Rosal, 7
33009 Oviedo
Tel: 22 94 30
Fax: 22 67 26

Officer-in-Charge
c/o British Institute
Plaza Nueva 8b
41001 Sevilla
Tel: 22 88 73
Telex: 72107 BRSEV/E
Fax: 21 03 23

Director Valencia
General San Martin 7
46004 Valencia
Tel: 351 88 18, 352 98 74
Fax: 352 86 88

Director Granada
C/Azhuma, 5
18005 Granada
Tel: 267913
Fax: 201905

Director Palma
British Institute
Goethe 1
07011 Palma de Mallorca
Tel: 45 48 55 712
Fax: 285009

Director Las Palmas
British Institute
Bravo Murillo 25
35003 Las Palmas de Gran Canaria
Tel: 368300
Fax: 382378

Sri Lanka
Director
49 Alfred House Gardens
Colombo 3
Tel: 581171/2/587078/9/580301

Librarian
178 DS Senanayake Vidiya
Kandy
Tel: 0823140, 0822410

Sudan
Director
14 Abu Sinn Stret
(PO Box 1253)
Khartoum
Tel: 74935, 80817
Telex: 23114 BCKHT SD

Swaziland
Director
c/o British High Commission
Allister Miller Street
Mbabane
(Private Bag, Mbabane)
Tel: 42581
Telex: 2006 WD BC

Sweden
Director
Skarpögatan 6
S-115-27 Stockholm
Tel: 6670 140
Telex: 19340 BRITEMB S (Embassy)
Fax: 6637 271

Tanzania
Director
Ohio Samora Avenue
(PO Box 9100)
Dar-es-Salaam
Tel: 22726/7, 33817/8/9
Telex: 41719 BRICO TZ
Fax: 22728

Thailand
Director
428 Rama 1 Road
Siam Square Soi Pathumwran
(c/o British Embassy BFPO 5)
Bangkok 10330
Tel: 252 6136/7/8, 252 6111
Telex: 72058 BRICOUN TH
Fax: 252 6111

Director Chiang Mai
198 Bumrungraj Road
Chiang Mai 5000
Tel: 242 103

Togo
see Ghana

Trinidad
see Caribbean

Tunisia
Director
c/o British Embassy
(BP 229)
5 Place de la Victoire
Tunis 1015 RP
Tel: 1259053
Telex: 13383 BC TUN
Fax: 353411

Turkey
Counsellor for British Council and Cultural Affairs
Kirlangic Sokak 9
Gazi Osman Pasa
Ankara 06700
Tel: 428 3165/9
Telex: 42049 IBIK TR
Fax: 427 6182

Consul for British Council and Cultural Affairs
Ors Turustik Is Merkezi
Istiklal Caddesi 251/253
Kat 2,3,5
Beyoglu
Istanbul 80060
Tel: 252 74774/8
Telex: 23283 IKIK TR
Fax: 2437682

Director
Izmir
1481. Sokak No 9
Alsancak
Izmir
Tel: 22 04 59
Fax: 22 35 38

Uganda
Director
c/o British High Commission
10/12 Parliament Avenue
(PO Box 7070)
Kampala
Tel: 257301/4/257054/9
Telex: 61202 UK REP KLA (High Commission)
Fax: 257304

United Arab Emirates
Director
Saadaqa Tower
near Emirates Plaza Hotel
Abu Dhabi
Tel: 788400
Telex: 24208 ADBRIC EM
Fax: 789516

Assistant Director
Tariq bin Zaid Street
near Rashid Hospital
(PO Box 1636)
Dubai
Tel: 370 109
Telex: 48096 DUBIC EM
Fax: 370703

United States of America
Cultural Attaché
British Embassy
3100 Massachusetts Avenue NW
Washington DC 20008
Tel: 462 1340
Telex: 892370 PRODROME B WSH
Fax: 8984255 (Embassy)

Venezuela
Director
Torre La Noria, Piso 6
Paseo Enrique Eraso
Las Mercedes/San Román
(Apartado 65131)
Caracas 1065
Tel: 915222, 915943, 915343
Telex: 24473 BRICO VC
Fax: 915943

Yemen
Director
Beit Al-Mottahar
Al-Bonia Street
Harat Handhal
(PO Box 2157)
Sana'a
Tel: 244154/6, 244121/2
Telex: 2748 BRCOUN YE
Fax: 274128

Yugoslavia
Director
Generala Zdanove
34-Mezanin
(Post Fah 248)
11001 Belgrade
Tel: 332 441, 327 910
Telex: 11032 BRIBEL YU
Fax: 631 664

Director Croatia
(See **Croatia**)

Zambia
Director
Heroes Place
Cairo Road
(PO Box 34571)
Lusaka
Tel: 223502, 228332
Telex: 40750 BRICO ZA
Fax: 214122

Librarian
Buteko Avenue
(PO Box 70415)
Ndola

Zimbabwe
Director
23 Jason Moyo Ave
(PO Box 664)
Harare
Tel: 790627/8/9, 793792/3,
790620
Telex: 24568
Fax: 4737

Appendix 2

USEFUL ADDRESSES FOR INFORMATION, ADVICE OR ASSISTANCE

*Offices in other cities also

Please send stamped addressed envelope or postal-reply coupon with enquiries to non-official organizations.

Accommodation bureaux, clubs and student welfare

Africa Centre
38 King Street
Covent Garden
London WC2E 8JT
Tel: (071) 836 1973

Live music, art gallery, African restaurant, bars, talks, evening classes, conferences, cultural events, rooms for hire, membership.

British Association of the Experiment in International Living
Otesaga
West Malvern Road
Malvern
Worcester WR14 4EN
Tel: (06845) 62577

CHAT (Counselling Help and Advice Together)
Royal College of Nursing
20 Cavendish Square
London W1M 0AB
Tel: (071) 409 3333

The Churches Commission on Overseas Students
1 Stockwell Green
London SW9 9HP
Tel: (071) 737 1101

Colin Winter Centre for Namibia
9 Cowley Road
Oxford OX4 1HP
Tel: (0865) 249977

Counselling and Education advice for Namibians.

Commission for Racial Equality
Elliot House
10/12 Allington Street
London SW1E 5EH
Tel: (071) 828 7022

Department of Health
Information Division
Hannibal House
Elephant and Castle
London SE1 6TE
Tel: (071) 972 2609

Department of Health
Division HAP4
Hannibal House
Elephant and Castle
London SE1 6TE
Tel: (071) 972 2630

English Speaking Union*
Dartmouth House
37 Charles Street
London W1X 8AB
Tel: (071) 493 3328

Educational charity

Hosting for Overseas Students (HOST)
18 Northumberland Avenue
London WC2N 5BJ
Tel: (071) 925 2595

Institute of Race Relations
2-6 Leeke Street
King's Cross Road
London WC1X 9HS
Tel: (071) 837 0041

International Family Service for Overseas Students
20 Waterloo Street
Birmingham B2 5TP
Tel: (021) 456 4000

International Friendship League
'Peace Haven'
3 Creswick Road
Acton
London W3 9HE
Tel: (081) 992 0221

International weekends and holidays.

Melbourne House
7/9 Heathville Road
Gloucester GL1 3DS
Tel: (0452) 418089

Has residential accommodation for individuals, groups and parties. Visitors to Britain particularly welcome.

International Social Service of UK
Cranmer House
39 Brixton Road
London SW9 6DD
Tel: (071) 735 8941

Monday to Friday 09.30 to 17.30

Interviews by appointment only. Case-work service for those whose problems cross national boundaries, an inter-national marriage counselling service and help for certain refugees. Cannot help with fees and grants.

International Society
84 Plymouth Grove
Manchester M13 9LW
Tel: (061) 273 1372

International Students House
229 Great Portland Street
London W1N 5HD
Tel: (071) 631 3223
Fax: (071) 636 5565

Daily 10.00 to 23.00

London's largest overseas student centre. Accommodation, club facilities, sports and social activities, advisory service.

International Voluntary Service*
188 Roundhay Road
Leeds LS8 5PL
Tel: (0532) 406787

Offers a range of voluntary service opportunities at summer work camps, organizes exchanges with voluntary organizations in Africa and Asia and involves overseas students living in Britain in its projects.

London Conference on Overseas Students
10 Spring Gardens
London SW1A 2BN
Tel: (071) 930 4527

London Council for the Welfare of Women and Girls/London YWCA
Accommodation and Advisory Service (LCWWG)
57 Great Russell Street
London WC1B 3BD
Tel: (071) 430 1524

Advisory service for hostel and other accommodation in the London area. Postal and telephone enquiries answered. Stamped, addressed envelopes or international reply coupons necessary for postal replies. Office open to personal callers Monday to Friday 11.00 to 15.00

London Voluntary Service Council
68 Chalton Street
London NW1 1JR
Tel: (071) 388 0241

National Association of Citizens Advice Bureaux
Middleton House
115-123 Pentonville Road
London N1 9LZ
Tel: (071) 833 2181

See telephone directory for local offices.

Liberty
21 Tabard Street
London SE1 4LA
Tel: (071) 403 3888
Formerly National Council for Civil Liberties

National Council of YMCAs
640 Forest Road
London E17 3DZ
Tel: (081) 520 5599

National Union of Students
461 Holloway Road
London N7 6LJ
Tel: (071) 272 8900

'OSPREY' International Student Advisory Council
4a Bruntsfield Crescent
Edinburgh EH10 4EZ
Tel: (031) 452 9243

Royal Association for Disability and Rehabilitation
25 Mortimer Street
London W1N 8AB
Tel: (071) 637 5400

Royal Commonwealth Society*
18 Northumberland Avenue
London WC2N 5BJ
Tel: (071) 930 6733

Library meetings. Programme open to Commonwealth students. Club facilities available to members. Details on request.

Royal Over-Seas League*
Over-Seas House
Park Place
St James's Street
London SW1A 1LR
Tel: (071) 408 0214
Telex: 268995 ROSL G
Fax: (071) 499 6738

Club facilities for Commonwealth members.

African Family Advisory Service
c/o Save the Children Fund

Cambridge House
Cambridge Grove
London W6 0LE

National Bureau for Students with Disabilities (SKILL)
336 Brixton Road
London SW9 7AA
Tel: (071) 274 0565

(Formerly known as the National Bureau for Handicapped Students (NHBS)). Provides information/advice to students with physical, sensory disabilities and with learning difficulties. Unable to give financial assistance.

United Kingdom Council for Overseas Student Affairs (UKCOSA)
9-17 St Albans Place
Islington
London N1 0NX
Tel: (071) 226 3762

Represents overseas students through affiliated organizations and universities.

United Nations Association
UNA Youth
3 Whitehall Court
London SW1A 2EL
Tel: (071) 930 2931

Universities and Colleges Christian Fellowship (UCCF)*
c/o YWCA Regional Office
Central Club
16/22 Great Russell Street
London WC1B 3LR
Tel: (071) 255 1443

Victoria League for Commonwealth Friendship*
18 Northumberland Avenue
London WC2N 5BJ

Student hostel in London, hospitality, holidays and social programme for students.

World University Service (UK)
20 Compton Terrace
London N1 2UN
Tel: (071) 226 6747

Activities include educational advice to refugees.

Young Men's Christian Association*
London Central YMCA
112 Great Russell Street
London WC1B 3NQ
Tel: (071) 637 1333

Youth Clubs UK
11 St Bride St
London EC4A 4AS
Tel: (071) 353 2366

Zebra Trust
25 Harrington Gardens
London SW7 4JT
Tel: (071) 373 7311

Monday to Friday 09.30 to 17.00

Administers Impala House, Jerome House, Sentosa House, Zebra House
Enquiries about accommodation should be made to the Warden (Addresses in Appendix 3.)

Educational organizations

Africa Educational Trust
38 King Street
London WC2E 8JS
Tel: (071) 836 5075

Educational and advice service for African students and the administration of small grants.

Monday to Friday 14.00 to 17.00

Art and Design Admissions Registry
Penn House
9 Broad Street
Hereford HR4 9AP
Tel: (0432) 266653

The Association for Recognised English Language Teaching Establishments in Britain (incorporating ARELS and FELCO)
2 Pontypool Place
Valentines Place
London SE1 8QF
Tel: (071) 242 3136

Publications listing members' services.

British Association of State Colleges in English Language Teaching (BASCELT)
c/o Cheltenham and Gloucestershire College of Higher Education
Cheltenham International Language Centre
Frances Close Hall
Swindon Road
Cheltenham
Gloucestershire GL50 4AZ
Tel: Cheltenham (0242) 532925
Fax: Cheltenham (0242) 532926

British Medical Association
Commonwealth and International Medical Advisory Bureau
Tavistock Square
London WC1H 9JP
Tel: (071) 387 4499

Monday to Friday 09.00 to 17.00

Provides a personal advisory and information service to its affiliated medical associations on short- or long-term visits to the United Kingdom.

CCETSW Information Service*
Derbyshire House
St Chad's Street
London WC1H 8AD
Tel: (071) 278 2455

Centralised Application to Nurse Training Clearing House (CATCH)
PO Box 21
Edinburgh EH2 1NT

Central Bureau for Educational Visits and Exchanges*
Seymour Mews House
Seymour Mews
London W1H 9PE
Tel: (071) 486 5101

Central Register and Clearing House Ltd
3 Crawford Place
London W1H 2BN

The Centre for Information on Language Teaching and Research (CILT)
Regent's College
Inner Circle
Regent's Park
London NW1 4NS
Tel: (071) 486 8221/4

Chartered Society of Physiotherapy
14 Bedford Row
London WC1
Tel: (071) 242 1941

Chief Nursing Officer
Welsh Office
Cathays Park
Cardiff CF1 3NG
Wales

Council for National Academic Awards (CNAA)
344/54 Gray's Inn Road
London WC1X 8BP
Tel: (071) 278 4411

Information on approved courses at colleges other than universities.

Department for Education
Sanctuary Buildings
Great Smith Street
Westminster
London SW1P 3BT
Tel: (071) 925 5000

Educational Grants Advisory Service
Family Welfare Association
501/5 Kingsland Road
London E8 4AU
Tel: (071) 254 6251

English National Board
Nurses' Central Clearing House
(PO Box 346)
Bristol BS99 7FB
Tel: (0272) 292282

English National Board for Nursing, Midwifery and Health Visiting
Victory House
170 Tottenham Court Road
London W1P 0HA
Tel: (071) 388 3131

English National Board for Nursing, Midwifery and Health Visiting
(PO Box 356)
Sheffield S8 0SJ
Tel: (0742) 555012

Graduate Teacher Training
Registry
PO Box 239
Cheltenham
Gloucestershire GL50 3SF

Health Education Authority
Hamilton House
Mabledon Place
London WC1H 9TX
Tel: (071) 387 9528

Independent Schools
Information Service
56 Buckingham Gate
London SW1E 6AG
Tel: (071) 630 8793/4

Recruitment Officer
National Board for Nursing,
Midwifery and Health Visiting
for Northern Ireland
RAC House
79 Chichester Street
Belfast BT1 4JE
Northern Ireland
Tel: (0232) 238152

Nurses' Central Clearing House
(PO Box 346)
Bristol BS99 7FB
Tel: (0272) 292282

National Board for Nursing and
Midwifery
21-22 Queens St
Edinburgh EH2 1JX
Tel: (031) 226 7371
Replaces the Nursing Adviser,
Scottish Health Service

Polytechnics Central Admission
System (PCAS)
The Fulton House
(PO Box 67)
Cheltenham
Gloucestershire
Tel: (0242) 227788

Regional Advisory Council for
Further Education*
232 Vauxhall Bridge Rd,
London SW1V 1AU
Tel: (071) 233 6199

Royal College of Nursing of the
United Kingdom
International Department
20 Cavendish Square
London W1M 0AB
Tel: (071) 409 3333

Professional organization and certified independent trade union, has student section.

Scottish Office Education
Department
New St Andrew's House
St James Centre
Edinburgh EH1 3TG
Tel: (031) 244 4442

United Kingdom Central
Council for Nursing, Midwifery
and Health Visiting (UKCC)
23 Portland Place
London W1N 3AS
Tel: (071) 637 7181

For overseas registration.

Universities Central Council of
Admissions (UCCA)
(PO Box 28)
Cheltenham
Gloucestershire
GL50 35A

Immigration and employment

Aliens' Registration Office*
(Metropolitan Police)
10 Lamb's Conduit Street
London WC1N 3NX
Tel: (071) 230 1208

Department of Economic
Development
Netherleigh House
Massey Avenue
Belfast BT4 2JP
Tel: (0232) 763244

Department of Employment
Caxton House
Tothill Street
London SW1H 9NF
Tel: (071) 273 6969

Belfast Immigration Office
Public Enquiry Office
Olive Tree House
Fountain Street
Belfast BT1 5ER
Tel: (0232) 322547

Tuesday, Wednesday and Thursday 14.00 to 16.00

Harwich Immigration Office
Parkeston Quay
Harwich CO12 4SX
Tel: (0603) 408859

Daily 14.00 to 16.00

Home Office (Immigration)*
Lunar House
40 Wellesley Road
Croydon CR9 2BY
Tel: (081) 686 0688

Joint Council for the Welfare of
Immigrants
115 Old Street
London EC1V 9JR
Tel: (071) 251 8706

Provides advice and representation on immigration and nationality problems.

Liverpool Immigration Office
Public Enquiry Office
Graeme House
Derby Square
Liverpool L2 7SF
Tel: (051) 236 8974

Tuesday to Friday 14.00 to 16.00

Norwich Immigration Office
Norwich Airport
Terminal Building
Norwich NR6 6JA
Tel: (0603) 408859
Wellesley Road,

Daily 14.30 to 17.00

Passport Office*
Clive House
70-78 Petty France
London SW1H 9HD
Tel: (071) 279 3434

United Kingdom Immigrant
Advisory Service (UKIAS)*
County House
2nd Floor
190 Great Dane Street
London SE1 4YB
Tel: (071) 357 6917

Women's Health

British Pregnancy Advisory
Service
7 Belgrave Road
Victoria
London SW1 1QB
Tel: (071) 222 0985

Advice on abortion, contraception, sterilization and pregnancy testing. 21 branches throughout the country. See telephone directory.

Family Planning Association
27-35 Mortimer Street
London W1N 7RJ
Tel: (071) 636 7866

Pregnancy Advisory Service
11/13 Charlotte Street
London W1P 1HN
Tel: (071) 637 8962

Advice on abortion, contraception, sterilization and pregnancy testing. See telephone directory for local offices.

Women's Health Concern
17 Earl's Terrace
London W8
Tel: (071) 938 3932

Women's Health
52 Featherstone Street
London EC1Y 8RT
Tel: (071) 251 6580

Travel

Association of British Travel Agents
55 Newman Street
London W1P 4AH
Tel: (071) 637 2444

Automobile Association
Fanum House
Basingstoke
Hants RG21 2EA
Tel: (0256) 493086

Advice on all aspects of motoring.

British Tourist Authority
Thames Tower
Blacks Road
Hammersmith
London W6 9EL
Tel: (081) 846 9000

Or contact:

The British Travel Centre
12 Regent's Street
London SW1 4PQ
Tel: (071) 730 3400

Department of Transport
(Driver and Vehicle Licensing Agency)
Longview Road
Morriston
Swansea SA6 7JL
Tel: (0792) 782363

HM Customs and Excise
New King's Beam House
22 Upper Ground
London SE1 9PJ
Tel: (071) 620 1313

Holiday Care Service
2 Old Bank Chambers
Station Road
Horley
Surrey RH6 9HW
Tel: (0293) 774535

Provides a free information service on accommodation and transport for holidays for any people who are physically disabled.

London Tourist Board
26 Grosvenor Gardens
London SW1W 0DU
Tel: (071) 730 3450
(071) 730 3488 (tourist information)

Written and telephone enquiries only.

Tourist Information Centre
Victoria Station Forecourt
London SW1
Tel: (071) 730 3488

Personal callers (every day). Telephone enquiries (Monday to Friday). Information on London and England only.

RAC
Marco Polo House
(PO Box 8)
3-5 Lansdowne Road
Croydon CR9 2JA
Tel: (071) 686 2314

Advice on all aspects of motoring.

Victoria Coach Station Ltd.
Buckingham Palace Road
London SW1W 9TP

Enquiries and tickets available at ticket counters only from 07.30 to 22.30.

The Youth Hostels Association
Trevelyan House
8 St Stephen's Hill
St Albans
Hertfordshire AL1 2DY
Tel: (0727) 55215

Appendix 3

STUDENT HOSTELS

M = men MC = married couples W = women Ch = children

London area

Acton YWCA (W)
East Acton Lane
London
W3 7LE
Tel: (081) 743 3285

AFSIL Ltd. (M, W, MC, Ch)
10 Endsleigh Gardens
London
WC1 0EH
Tel: (071) 388 7144

Alliance Club (M)
44-45 Newington Green
London
N16 9QH
Tel: (071) 226 6085

Ashley House (W)
YWCA
12-14 Endsleigh Gardens
London
WC1H OEH
Tel: (071) 387 3378

Barnet Overseas Students Housing Association (MC, Ch)
Nansen Village
21 Woodside Avenue
London
N12 8AQ
Tel: (081) 445 8644

Bernard Johnson House (MC, Ch)
78 Fortis Green
London
N2 9EX
Tel: (081) 883 4336

Catholic Students International (M)
International Chaplaincy
34 Adolphus Road
London
N4 2AY
Tel: (081) 802 9673

Centre Français (M, W)
61/9 Chepstow Place
London
W2 4TR
Tel: (071) 221 8134

Chester House Hostel (M, W)
1 Chester House
Pages Lane
Muswell Hill
London
N10 1PR
Tel: (081) 883 8204

Christian Alliance Centre (M, W)
Secker Street
London
SE1 8UF
Tel: (071) 633 0128

Clubland Methodist Hostel (M, W)
56 Camberwell Road
London
SE5 0EN
Tel: (071) 701 0233

Croydon YMCA (M, W)
1 Lansdowne Road
Croydon
CR0 2BX
Tel: (081) 681 3381

Gilmore House (MC, Ch)
113 Clapham Common
North Side
London
SW4 9SJ
Tel: (071) 228 2130

Helen Graham House (M, W)
YWCA
57 Great Russell Street
London
WC1B 3BD
Tel: (071) 430 0834

Hornsey YMCA (M, W)
184 Tottenham Lane
London
N8 8SG
Tel: (081) 340 2345

Impala House (M, MC, Ch)
8 Chalcot Square
London
NW1 8YB
Tel: (071) 722 4643

International Students' House (M, W, MC, Ch)
229 Great Portland Street
London
W1N 5HD
Tel: (071) 631 3223

International Students' Housing Society (M, W, MC, Ch)
International House
109 Brookhill Road
Woolwich
London
SE18 6RZ
Tel: (081) 854 1418/9

Jerome House (M, W, MC, Ch)
19 Harrington Gardens
London
SW7 4LS
Tel: (071) 373 0278

Princess House YWCA (W)
39 Ennismore Gardens
London
SW7 1AG
Tel: (071) 584 3060

Shared accommodation only.

Kingston upon Thames Churches Housing Association (M, W,)
20 Thetford Road
New Malden
Surrey
KT3 5DT
Tel: (081) 949 0728

Lee Abbey International Students Club (M, W)
57-67 Lexham Gardens
London
W8 6JJ
Tel: (071) 373 7242

Lillian Penson Hall (University of London) (M, W, MC)
Talbot Square
London
W2 1TT
Tel: (071) 262 2081

London Friendship Centre (M, W)
'Peace Haven'
3 Creswick Road
London
W3 9HE
Tel: (081) 992 0221

London Goodenough Trust (M, W, MC)
Mecklenburgh Square
London
WC1N 2AB
Tel: (071) 837 8888

William Goodenough House (M, W, MC, Ch)
Mecklenburgh Square
London
WC1N 2AB
Tel: (071) 837 8888

Fellowship House (M, W, MC)
Mecklenburgh Square
London
WC1N 2AB
Tel: (071) 837 8888
Postgraduate students from Commonwealth, ex-Commonwealth, USA and Europe.

Malaysia Housing Society (M, W, MC, Ch)
Sentosa House
15/19 Upper Montague Street
London
W1H 1RR
Tel: (071) 402 5757

International House
2 Inverness Terrace
London
W2 3HY
Tel: (071) 229 5101

Park House YWCA (W)
227 Earls Court Road
London
SW5 9BL
Tel: (071) 373 2851

Religious of Mary Immaculate (W)
'Struan'
44 Augustus Road
London
SW19 6NB
Tel: (081) 788 9477

Romford YMCA (M, W)
Rush Green Road
Romford, Essex
RM7 0PH
Tel: (0708) 766211

Rothamsted Overseas Housing Association (M, W, MC, Ch)
Rothamsted Experimental Station
Harpenden
Hertfordshire
AL5 2JQ
Tel: (05827) 63133

Salvation Army (W)
Hopetown
60 Old Montague Street
London E1
Tel: (071) 246 1004

Sisters of St Dorothy International Students Hostel (W)
Frognal House
99 Frognal
London
NW3 6XR
Tel: (071) 794 6893/8095

London Student Housing (M, W, MC,)
Friendship House
1 St Nicholas Glebe
Rectory Lane
Tooting
London
SW17 9QH
Tel: (081) 672 2262

Also at:
Friendship House (M, MC,Ch)
13/17 Breakspears Road
Brockley
London
SE4 1XW
Tel: (081) 691 8111

Stockwell YMCA (M, W)
King George's House
40 Stockwell Road
London
SW9 9ES
Tel: (071) 274 7861

Victoria League Students House (M, W)
55 Leinster Square
London
W2 4PU
Tel: (071) 229 3961

Commonwealth students under the age of 30.

Waltham Forest YMCA (M, W)
642 Forest Road
Walthamstow
London E17 3EF
Tel: (081) 520 0931/2

Watford YMCA (M, W)
Charter House
Charter Place
Watford
WD1 2RT
Tel: (0923) 233034

William Temple House (M, W)
29 Trebovir Road
London
SW5 9NF
Tel: (071) 373 6962

Wimbledon YMCA (M, W)
200 The Broadway
Wimbledon
London
SW19 1RY
Tel: (081) 542 9055

YMCA (M, W)
112 Great Russell Street
London
WC1B 3NO
Tel: (071) 637 1333

Zebra House (M, W)
3 Marloes Road
London
W8 6LH
Tel: (071) 373 2127

Hostels for nationals

Denmark
Danish YMCA
43 Maresfield Gardens
London
NW3 5TF
Tel (071) 435 2007

Preference given to Danish men and women. All shared rooms. Tube station; Finchley Road.

France
The French Centre
29 The Boltons
London
SW10
Tel: (071) 370 3649

Men and women of all nationalities. Tube station; Earls Court.

Germany
German YMCA
35 Craven Terrace
Lancaster Gate
London
W2 3EL
Tel: (071) 723 9276

Men and women of all nationalities. Tube station: Earls Court

India
Indian Students Hostel (YMCA)
41 Fitzroy Square
London
W1P 6AQ
Tel: (071) 387 0411

Men and women of all nationalities. Tube station; Great Portland Street or Warren Street.

Malaysia
Malaysia Hall
46 Bryanston Square
London
W1H 8AJ
Tel: (071) 723 9484

Only Malaysian men and women. Office — 44 Bryanston Square, hostel — 46 Bryanston Square. Tube station; Marble Arch.

Muslim Hostel
38 Tapestry Road
London
NW2 4JD
Tel: (081) 452 9340

Muslim men only. Tube station: Kilburn.

Poland
Polish YMCA
46/7 Kensington Gardens Square
London
W2 4BQ
Tel: (071) 229 4295

Men and women of all nationalities. Tube station: Bayswater or Queensway.

Sweden
Enquiries to:
Swedish Church
6 Harcourt Street
London
W1H 2BD
Tel: (071) 732 5681

Tube station: Edgware Road. Accommodation in emergencies only.

Other hostels in the United Kingdom

Aberdeen
Cameron House (W)
2-4 Charlotte Street
Aberdeen
AB1 1LR
Tel: (0224) 634966

Aviemore
Torr Lodge (M)
Morlich Court
Aviemore
PH22 1SL
Tel: (0479) 810150

Bath
City of Bath YMCA (M, W)
YMCA International House
Broad Street Place
Bath
Avon
BA1 5LH
Tel: (0225) 460471

Belfast
YWCA (M, W)
Queen Mary's Hostel
70 Fitzwilliam Street
Belfast
BT9 6AX
Tel: (0232) 240439

YWCA Hostel (M, W)
3-5 Malone Road
Belfast
BT9 6RT
Tel: (0232) 668347

Birkenhead
YMCA (M, W)
56 Whetstone Lane
Birkenhead
L41 2TJ
Tel: (051) 647 8123

Birmingham
Kingsmead College (M, W)
997 Bristol Road
Selly Oak
Birmingham
B29 6LP
Tel: (021) 472 0013

Methodist International House (M, W, MC *no* Ch)
52 Oakfield Road
Selly Park
Birmingham
B29 7EQ
Tel: (021) 472 0109

Methodist Overseas Guest House (M, W, MC, Ch)
College Walk
Selly Oak
Birmingham
B29 6LF
Tel: (021) 472 0163

YMCA (M, W)
300 Reservoir Road
Erdington
Birmingham
B23 6DB
Tel: (021) 373 1937

Bournemouth
YMCA (M, W)
56 Westover Road
Bournemouth
BH1 2BS
Tel: (0202) 290451

Bristol
Girls Friendly Society (W)
Townsend House
Pump Lane
Redcliff
Bristol
BS1 6NW
Tel: (0272) 273844

Hodgkin House (M, W)
3/7 Meridian Place
Clifton
Bristol
BS8 1JG
Tel: (0272) 734543 (Warden)

Methodist International House (M, W)
Rodney House
Clifton Down Road
Clifton
Bristol
BS8 4AL
Tel: (0272) 735179 (Warden)

YWCA
15 Berkeley Square
Clifton
Bristol
Tel: (0272) 277057 (Warden)

Zebra Trust (MC, Ch)
Zebra House
9 Miles Road
Clifton
Bristol
BS8 2JN

Cambridge
YMCA (M, W, MC)
Gonville Place
Cambridge
CB1 1ND
Tel: (0223) 356998

Cardiff
YMCA (M, W)
The Walk
Roath
Cardiff
CF2 3AG
Tel: (0222) 497044

Cheltenham
YMCA (M, W)
6 Vittoria Walk
Cheltenham
GL50 1TP
Tel: (0242) 524024

Dalkeith
Lauder Lodge (M)
Newmills Road
Dalkeith
Midlothian
EH22 1DX
Tel: (031) 6601069

Derby
YMCA (M, W)
London Road
Wilmorton
Derby
DE2 8UT
Tel: (0332) 572076

Edinburgh
Caledonia House (W)
41 Lothian Road
Edinburgh
Tel: (031) 229 1747

Lauriston (W)
77 Lauriston Place
Edinburgh
EH3 9HY
Tel: (031) 228 3132

Scottish Council YWCA Housing Society (W and Ch)
22 Rutland Square
Edinburgh
EH1 2BB
Tel: (031) 229 9765

Flats for overseas students' families.

YWCA
22 Rutland Square
Edinburgh
EH1 2BB
Tel: (031) 229 9765

Exeter
YMCA (M)
5 Heavitree Rd
Exeter
EX1 2LD
Tel: (0392) 410530

Glasgow
YMCA (M, W, MC)
David Naismith Court
33 Petershill Drive
Glasgow
G21 4QQ
Tel: (041) 558 6166

YMCA (M, W)
Lindsay House
Kittoch Street
East Kilbride
Glasgow
G74 4JN
Tel: (041) 558 6166

Nautical College (M, W)
21 Thistle Street
Glasgow
G5 9XB
Tel: (041) 429 3201

Gloucester
Gloucester Friendship Centre (M, W, MC, Ch)
'Melbourne House'
7/9 Heathville Road
Gloucester
GL1 3DS
Tel: (0452) 418089

Grimsby
Grimsby Cleethorpes and District YMCA (M, W)
Peaks Lane
Grimsby
DN32 9ET
Tel: (0472) 357788

Hull
Hull Methodist International House (M, W, MC)
96-8 Westbourne Avenue
Hull HU5 3HY
Tel: (0482) 42104

Hull International House (M, W, MC)
96/8 Westbourne Avenue
Hull
HU5 3HY
Tel: (0482) 42104

Inverness
Flora Macdonald Residence (W)
30 Old Edinburgh Road
Inverness
IV2 3HJ
Tel: (0463) 233080/236609

Ipswich
YMCA (M, W)
2 Wellington Street
Ipswich
2P1 2NU
Tel: (0473) 252456

Kirkaldy
Kirkaldy YWCA Residence
9 The Esplanade
Kirkaldy
KY1 1H
Tel: (0592) 260963

Leicester
Heathfield House YWCA (M, W)
236 London Road
Leicester
LE2 1RH
Tel: (0533) 705083

Liverpool
YPHA (M, W, MC)
7th Floor
Wellington Buildings
The Strand
Liverpool
L2 0PP
Tel: (051) 227 3716

YMCA (M, W, MC)
56-60 Mount Pleasant
Liverpool L3 5FH
Tel: (051) 709 9516

Mildmay House (M, W)
6 Blackburne Place
Liverpool
L8 7PQ
Tel: (051) 709 1417

Loughborough
International Centre (Loughborough) Ltd. (M, W, MC, Ch)
94 Leicester Road
Loughborough
LE11 2AQ
Tel: (0509) 216288

Manchester
Methodist International House (M, W)
68 Daisy Bank Road
Victoria Park
Manchester
M14 5QP
Tel: (061) 224 8041

Alexandra House (W)
73 Carlton Road
Manchester
M16 8BD
Tel: (061) 226 2768

Newcastle upon Tyne
YWCA (M, W)
Jesmond House
Clayton Road
Newcastle upon Tyne
NE2 1UJ
Tel: (091) 281 5466

Norwich
YMCA (M, W)
48 St Giles Street
Norwich
NR2 1LP
Tel: (0603) 20269

Nottingham
YMCA (M, W)
4 Shakespeare Street
Nottingham
NG1 4FG
Tel: (0602) 473068

Oxford
British Council Hostel (M, W, MC)
47 St John Street
Oxford
OX1 2LQ
Tel: (0865) 54725

YWCA (W)
133 Woodstock Road
Oxford
OX2 6HW
Tel: (0865) 52021

Plymouth
YWCA (M, W)
9-13 Lockyer Street
Plymouth
PL1 2QQ
Tel: (0752) 660321

Portsmouth and Southsea
YMCA (M, W)
Penny Street
Portsmouth
PO1 2NN
Tel: (0705) 864341

Reading
Foley Hall (M, MC)
58/60 London Road
Reading
RG1 5AS
Tel: (0734) 872280

Trinity Hall (M, W)
South Street
Reading
RG1 4QU
Tel: (0734) 391013

YMCA (M, W)
Marlborough House
34 Parkside Road
Reading
RG3 2DD
Tel: (0734) 575746

Sheffield
YMCA (M, W, MC)
20 Victoria Road
Sheffield
S10 2DL
Tel: (0742) 662221

Southampton
University of Southampton (M, W)
Highfield
Southampton
SO9 5NH
Tel: (0703) 595000

YWCA (M, W)
5 Bellevue Road
Southampton
SO9 5ZG
Tel: (0703) 227155

YMCA (M, W)
George Williams House
Cranbury Place
The Avenue
Southampton
SO2 0LG
Tel: (0703) 221202

Taunton
YWCA Residential Club (M, W)
18 Mary Street
Taunton
Somerset
TA1 3PE
Tel: (0823) 284682

West Bromwich
West Bromwich and District YMCA (M, W)
John Lees House
38 Carters Green
West Bromwich
West Midlands
B70 9LG
Tel: (021) 553 4211/2

Wolverhampton
YWCA (M, W)
The Lindens &
International House (M, W)
100 Penn Road
Wolverhampton
WV3 0DW
Tel: (0902) 23733 The Lindens
(0902) 24596 International House

York
York Housing Association Ltd (M, W, MC, Ch)
2 Newgate
York
YO1 2LA
Tel: (0904) 636061

Appendix 4

FURTHER READING

Below is a selection of useful books on Britain and British education which will be available at bookshops and libraries in Britain. Education reference books are also available for consultation at British Council offices overseas and in London; a smaller selection is available at the Council's UK regional offices.

General

Angel, H. & others. *The natural history of Great Britain and Ireland* Peerage Books 1985 (paperback) £5.95
Britain: an official handbook HMSO: Foreign & Commonwealth Office 1991 £15.95
Britain at your leisure Automobile Association 1988 £8.95
Fodor's Affordable Great Britain – How to see the best for less. Fodor's Travel Publication 1992 £8.99
Fodor's Great Britain Random Century annual 1991 £12.99
Austerberry, Watson & Moth. *Guide to Women's Hostels in London SHAC* 1983 £2.50
London briefing: a guide to leisure for overseas students London Conference on Overseas Students (in association with the British Council) annual free
Mikes, G. *How to be a Brit* Penguin 1986 £4.99
Sampson, G. *The concise Cambridge history of English literature* Cambridge University Press 1970 £22.50
Stay with a British family British Tourist Authority annual free
Time Out guide to London for visitors Penguin 1992 £9.99
Freemans. *Student Cook Book* Collins & Brown 1990, £4.99.
Young Britain British Tourist Authority annual free

Education

Awards for commonwealth university academic staff Association of Commonwealth Universities biennial 1989£14.75
International guide to qualifications in education Mansell 1991 (in association with the British Council) £90.
British qualifications Kogan Page Ltd. annual (hardback) £32.50
British Universities guide to graduate study Association of Commonwealth Universities annual 1990 £19.95
Compendium of advanced courses in colleges of further and higher education London and South Eastern Advisory Council for Education and Training annual 1991 £5.50
Degree course guides: 2 volumes. Hobsons Press (for CRAC) biennial £54.95 per vol
Directory of further education Hobsons Press (for CRAC) annual
(paperback) £44.95
(hardback) £59.45
Directory of postgraduate and post-experience courses Council for National Academic Awards annual free
Education information sheets The British Council free
Education yearbook Longman annual £57.50
English studies information sheets The British Council free
Financial aid for first-degree study at Commonwealth universities Association of Commonwealth Universities biennial 1989 £4.50
Floodlight: ILEA guide to part-time day and evening classes in Inner London Inner London Education Authority annual £1.50
Graduate studies Hobsons Press (for CRAC) annual £87.95
Higher education in the United Kingdom Longman (for the Association of Commonwealth Universities) annual 1991 £14.95
Parents' guide to independent schools SFIA Educational Trust Ltd annual 1991 £25.00
Polytechnic courses handbook Committee of Directors of Polytechnics annual £12.75

Further Reading

Scholarships guide for Commonwealth postgraduate students Association of Commonwealth Universities biennial 1988 £13.50
The student book: the applicant's guide to universities, polytechnics and UK colleges Macmillan Press annual 1992 £11.99
Study abroad Unesco biennial (available through HMSO in the UK) 1991 £14.00
Which degree?: 5 volumes. Newpoint Publishers 1990 £9.95 per vol
University entrance: the official guide Association of Commonwealth Universities annual 1991 £12.95